# *OXFORDSHIRE*

Edited by Jenny Edwards

First published in Great Britain in 1998 by
*POETRY NOW YOUNG WRITERS*
1-2 Wainman Road, Woodston,
Peterborough, PE2 7BU
Telephone (01733) 230748

All Rights Reserved

*Copyright Contributors 1998*

HB ISBN 0 75430 050 1
SB ISBN 0 75430 051 X

# *FOREWORD*

With over 63,000 entries for this year's Cosmic competition, it has proved to be our most demanding editing year to date.

We were, however, helped immensely by the fantastic standard of entries we received, and, on behalf of the Young Writers team, thank you.

The Cosmic series is a tremendous reflection on the writing abilities of 8-11 year old children, and the teachers who have encouraged them must take a great deal of credit.

We hope that you enjoy reading *Cosmic Oxfordshire* and that you are impressed with the variety of poems and style with which they are written, giving an insight into the minds of young children and what they think about the world today.

# CONTENTS

## Edward Feild School

Freeland CE Primary School

| | |
|---|---|
| Miranda Scott | 87 |
| Hannah McNeil | 88 |
| Jennifer Collett | 88 |
| Tamsin Haigh | 89 |
| Josh Mutlow | 89 |
| Darius Hodaei | 90 |
| Beth Hewitt | 91 |
| Catherine Hall | 92 |
| Paul Jacobs | 92 |
| Lucy McGregor | 93 |

Great Milton CE Primary School

| | |
|---|---|
| Laura Watts | 94 |
| Adam Buck | 94 |
| Simon Toms | 95 |
| James Enser | 96 |
| Simon Taylor | 96 |
| Laura Robinson | 97 |
| Jenny Flowers | 98 |
| Fabienne Morgan | 98 |
| Matthew Winyard | 99 |
| Aaron Johns | 99 |

Millbrook Primary School

| | |
|---|---|
| Jennie Green | 100 |
| Lucy Cripps | 101 |
| Craig Gillott | 102 |
| Jenny Yates | 102 |
| Laura Yates | 103 |
| Jessica Dancy | 104 |
| Lauren Marie Chessum | 105 |
| Rory McLean | 106 |
| Stefan Overy | 106 |
| Kerry Revell | 107 |
| Claire Morris | 108 |
| Hollie Sawyer | 108 |
| Shannon Lee Hetherington | 109 |

St Andrew's School

St Mary's CE Primary School

St Mary's RC Primary School

Uffington Primary School

| | |
|---|---|
| Scott Macdonald | 174 |
| Charlotte Rayner | 174 |
| Charlotte Holley | 175 |
| Karen Cooper | 175 |
| Jack Baily | 176 |
| Louise Sworn | 176 |
| Sophie Bowsher | 177 |
| Emma Rayner | 178 |

## Wantage CE Junior School

| | |
|---|---|
| Margaret Tingey | 178 |
| Laura Hickman | 179 |
| Rebecca Sutton | 180 |
| Sam Fox | 180 |
| Alan Easton | 181 |
| Stewart Hannah | 181 |
| Thomas Harris | 182 |
| Rachel Bowers | 182 |
| Lee Rutter | 183 |
| Ben Boden | 183 |
| Sam Withnall | 184 |
| Michael Donovan | 184 |
| Natasha Valentine | 185 |
| Jenny Leslie | 186 |
| Andrew Boyle | 186 |
| Cheryl Chittock | 187 |
| Nadia Walton | 188 |
| Kim Kelly | 189 |
| Christopher Fellingham | 190 |
| Jordan Molyneux | 190 |
| Harry Coules | 191 |
| Daniel Monnery | 191 |
| Ross Kerr | 192 |
| Andrew Bennett | 192 |
| Hannah Blow | 193 |
| Annie Berrett | 193 |
| David Oakes | 194 |
| Stuart Chaplin | 194 |

# THE POEMS

## SAVE THE WORLD

Stop the fighting.
Stop the guns
Talk don't use bombs
Save our world
Don't let it go.

*Zara Lee Bookham*


## COSMIC

Millions, billions, trillions
of stars
millions, billions, trillions
of light years away
flashing
blinding
bursting
shooting across the universe
passing other planets
as they zoom by
glittering
flickering
shining high
darting to and fro
extinguishing their light
as they go far

We watch in wonder
as new stars appear
and old ones fade
just like life
here on Earth.

*Theodora Joy-Jarvis  (11)*
*Beckley CE School*

## COSMIC

Hurtling through space at the speed of light
Towards the black hole that was once the sun.
Slowing, ever slowing,
Trying with all the power to stop,
But failing.

I try again,
To reverse out of the black hole.
But still,
The ship hurtles forward, still at the speed of light,
Helped by the gravitational pull of the black hole.

Faster, ever faster,
More out of control every second,
While the universe gets smaller,
The ship is sucked closer, closer to the centre
                                    of the black hole.

Panic stops . . .

      As I face reality,

           My ship is compressed smaller
           and smaller, and I am dying,
                  ever dying.

*Alexander Shearn  (9)*
*Beckley CE School*

## COSMIC

C osmic stars everywhere.
O n every planet they must go.
S trange things in the cosmic air.
M onsters stare here and there.
I ncredible things flying everywhere.
C osmic shooting stars are passing by.

S hivering Pluto next to Neptune
T ales of aliens carry on.
A stronauts on the moon.
R ushing in their ships to and fro.
S topping on the Earth below.

*Craig Drew  (10)*
*Beckley CE School*

## COSMIC

Shaking tremendously
towards the hidden galaxy
unbearable to see
unbearable to hear.
Orbiting planets from side to side
until we reach the shiny system.
We slow down at too quick a pace
I close my eyes and dream away.

*Daniel Clark  (10)*
*Beckley CE School*

# COSMIC

I'm lying on my bed on a cold winter's night,
Staring out of my window watching stars in flight.
I see a shooting star fly by,
With a blue and red tail flashing in the sky.

In a dream I see Saturn and Mars,
I touch moondust and glide past the stars
There's an American flag flying on the moon,
It's just like the one in my friend's room.
*It's cosmic! It's cosmic!*

Suddenly my dreams turn into a nightmare,
I am too near the sun,
No longer am I having fun.
It's scorching hot I feel blisters on my face
This is my last journey into cosmic space.

**Charlotte Pauling  (11)**
**Beckley CE School**


# COSMIC

Cosmic power is flowing out in space,
Oxygen is nowhere to be found,
Saturn is circling around in space,
Mars is turning redder by the minute,
In space, aliens are having a war,
Cosmic power is nowhere to be found
                                            anymore.

**Dale White  (10)**
**Beckley CE School**

## COSMIC

Sitting at my window
Looking at the sky
Wanting to get up there
'Can't wait' says I.
It's cosmic
*Cosmic!*

Soaring in my spacecraft
Seeing aliens fly,
They're blobby green and gooey
And covered in eyes.
It's cosmic
*Cosmic!*

Mummy calling 'Teatime'
Me sniffing saying 'Bye.'
Sitting in the dining room
Doing up my tie,
It was cosmic
*Cosmic!*

**Sarah Breach  (10)**
**Beckley CE School**


## COSMIC

Cosmic cauliflowers coming soon,
On my ears and in my hair,
Soon be here, soon be there,
Millions and millions of underwear,
In my face and in my feet,
Cosmic cauliflowers are really neat.

**Timmy Bartlett  (10)**
**Beckley CE School**

# COSMIC

A little boy stood in his garden,
He heard a 'burp' and then a 'pardon',
He saw a spaceship come down from the sky,
He looked up and said 'It can fly!'

Ugly aliens came down from the ship,
They said 'Bloomy bloo!' and 'Bleep, bleep, blip!'
They had big fat noses and mouths as wide,
The boy laughed a lot and then he sighed.

The aliens had left back to the ship,
With guns at hand and a 'Blonkety blip'!
The spaceship roared with a puff of smoke,
It zoomed off leaving no time to choke.
Soon it was just a dot in the sky,
The boy cried with a solemn 'Bye bye.'

*Nicholas Richard Moore (9)*
*Beckley CE School*


## MY FAMILY

My sister sits in the corner,
cosy in her chair,
engrossed in her reading,
but I couldn't care,
I turn to watch my brother,
doing karate chops in the air,
my dad looks like a big bear,
standing watching me from over there,
my mum sits in her chair,
fiddling with my hair,
I do love my family.

*Chelsea Smith (9)*
*Brookside CP School*

## MY DAY

In the morning I am a grouch,
And at night I always slouch.

My mum always bosses me around,
Shouting 'Get out of your night-gown!'

Then I eat my Malt Wheats,
Which my sister never eats.

Then I brush my scratty hair,
Which I never do with care.

I am on my way to Brookside school,
Tuesday means the swimming pool!

And then next I do my writing,
All about Saxons and Vikings,

At twelve o'clock I have my lunch,
It really is a tasty bunch!

At break our game is 'forty forty in',
And for our base we use a smelly bin.

Time to go home, I grab my bag,
*Pizza* for tea, boy am I glad!

If my sisters and I do not have a fight,
For dessert we will have Angel Delight!

*Emily Cox  (8)*
*Brookside CP School*

## WHAT IN THE WORLD AM I?

I am a millionaire,
I wear seven hats,
I play the oboe,
I can't play football,
What am I?

*I haven't a clue!*

**Andrew Payne (9)**
**Brookside CP School**


## ONE CAT

We used to have two cats
We were living normally
until it happened
He was poorly already
his name was Sam
He loved us especially Squeak and Frisby
They all played together
he jumped on my bed
and fell asleep
He chased birds
he went through the hedges
round Nanny Cooper's
she gave him food
I loved him
But they put him down
I still love him
But now
            we have one cat.

**Alison Beacham (8)**
**Chadlington CE Primary School**

## THE WISE OWL

The wise owl
glides through the air
The wise owl
eats mice and seeds
The wise owl
sleeps in a tree
The wise owl
flies to safety
The wise owl
gets shot and bleeds
The wise owl
isn't wise anymore
The wise owl
is dead.

*Kylie Plumbridge  (10)*
*Chadlington CE Primary School*


## THE SAFETY PIN

Everyone knows now,
It's gone round the school.
It's all Anna's fault.
I'm angry and embarrassed
She promised not to tell anyone
But she did.
Amanda's been following me.
I am really annoyed now.
I didn't think they'd notice that
*I had a safety pin in the back of my trousers.*
I'll never live it down.

*Kayleigh Down  (11)*
*Chadlington CE Primary School*

## POUNDING ANGER

I'm choking with *anger*
I'm frustrated like hell
I'm foaming at the mouth
It's all because of . . . yes,
                    *my sister!*

I go up to my room and just lie on my bed
I'm still swearing inside me
I've got a whirlwind of anger going
                    round in my head.

I'm plotting my revenge
I'm rubbing my hands
My sister won't last long
Her days are numbered
10, 9, 8, 7, 6, 5, 4, 3, 2, 1 . . .

*Kyran Hill  (9)*
*Chadlington CE Primary School*


## HEADACHE OF SADNESS

It's like a boomerang of sadness someone has thrown
and it is spinning in my head
banging on each side giving me a headache of sadness
It's like Niagara Falls running down my face
It's like my heart has exploded and my
sadness has spread all around my body
Now my sadness has joined with anger
It's like I have drowned in sadness
It's like some evil witches have made a sadness potion
and have given it to my heart and it
                    has exploded with sadness.

*Becky Woodall  (10)*
*Chadlington CE Primary School*

## The Hiccup

*Hic . . . Hic . . .*

They've started again,
How can I stop them?
Gargling water?
People going *'Boo!'*

Have they stopped?

*Hic . . . Hic . . .*

Oh no!
How can I stop them?
Drinking water at the same time
as standing on my head . . . ?
. . . silence for 1 minute . . .
. . . silence for 2 minutes . . .

*Hic . . .*

*Oh no!*

**Donna Allen  (11)**
**Chadlington CE Primary School**


## Philosophy And Apple Pie

Who are you and who am I?
Do we always have to die?
What do we feel?
And are we real?
How do you make apple pie?

**Lauren Allan  (11)**
**Chadlington CE Primary School**

## WHEN I'M OLD

When I'm old I'll smoke
And have my hair red, blue, orange
And pierce my tongue
And wear blue and green shoes
And wear fancy clothing
And have my hair long
And wear long nails
And be a gladiator like Wolf Man.

But now I will be nice to people
And play with children
And invite people for tea
And have a celebration.

But now I will be careful in case
My hair and nails grow longer
And I smoke
And be careful
Not to be like Wolf Man . . .

*Lisa Griffiths  (10)*
*Chadlington CE Primary School*


## THE ROAD

There was a road
There was a diamond road
There was a sparkly diamond road
There was a puddle
It was black
In the puddle
In the black puddle
There was
           *nothing.*

*Lettie Marie Kerry  (9)*
*Chadlington CE Primary School*

## AUTUMN

Red orange and yellow leaves
Swish and swirl in the wind.
Badgers plod in and out
of their holes
carrying food.
The sound of fireworks
sends cats sprawling.
Raindrops go pitter patter
pitter patter
on the window.
Squirrels sit on branches
munching nuts.

*Will Phipps  (8)*
*Chadlington CE Primary School*

## WHAT'S THAT IN THE UNDERGROWTH?

What's that in the undergrowth over there?
It looks green and orange
in the undergrowth over there.
Just look at it dripping
in the undergrowth over there.
Shall we go
to the undergrowth over there?
No - Just run for it.

> *Run, run away.*

*Sam Bunney  (8)*
*Chadlington CE Primary School*

## CHEETAH

The cheetah
is coming
prowling
through
the long
grass
leaping
now faster
and faster
chasing the impalas.
He catches one.
He drags it
up a tree
   and devours it.

*Richard Ingram (8)*
*Chadlington CE Primary School*


## POEM

A poem's like an alphabet in the sky
Or maybe flying butterflies
      with little letters on their wings.
Or maybe people walking into town
Or maybe winning the bingo game
Or maybe a tingle in my body
Or . . .
Or . . .
I now know what a poem is like!
A poem!

*Amanda Hunt (9)*
*Chadlington CE Primary School*

## STUCK!

'Right then, class, write a poem,' said my teacher
My heart was shocked
But happy, in a way,
But I was stuck,
Completely, utterly, splutterly stuck.
Who does she think she is?
No practise. Nothing!
It was like a big wall was blocking me
From getting to the other side.
Or . . . a giant wearing Doc Marten's
Or . . . a pot of gold which refills your mind
With different things.
Or . . . a sea of hungry sharks.
Wait there! That's not going to happen!
I've had a thought.
*Phew!*

***Thomas Cleevely  (10)***
***Chadlington CE Primary School***


## THE FIRST JAGUAR

Thunder was rolling, lightning was smashing,
The wind was whirling, trees were crashing,
Twigs were snapping, leaves were prancing,
Rain was pouring, clouds were dancing,
An earthquake was cutting the world apart;
A funny feeling cut through my heart;
A gigantic mountain rose up like a wave
And in the middle there was a cave
And out of the cave . . . came . . . a
                            *Jaguar!*

***Matthew Bunney  (11)***
***Chadlington CE Primary School***

## A Bird Of Prey

There the bird perches.
Here a shrew
scuttles on the ground.
As the bird
swoops and swerves,
the creature goes to hide
among the rushes
green and fresh,
just the place to hide.
The bird
tries to find
the creature small.
She does not succeed
      . . . this time.

*Eleanor Craddock  (9)*
*Chadlington CE Primary School*


## Next Saturday

On the 15th November
I'm going to play against Carterton.
Last time we played them
It was 2-1
To them.
This time
We're going to win
I'm going to score 2 hat tricks.
I'm going to play brilliantly.
I'm going to *win!*

*Andy Gardener  (8)*
*Chadlington CE Primary School*

## What Is A Poem?

What is a poem?
A poem is a thousand words
A picture in disguise.

A poem is a dream come true
A wonderful thing in my mind.

A poem is so crystal clear
A part of my life.

A poem is as soft as snow
A bright sparkling light.

A poem never ends.
It will always be alive.

*Sara Payne  (10)*
*Chadlington CE Primary School*


## Embarrassment

I was playing a game.
We lost 10-0.
I felt really embarrassed.
I hate losing.
When I lose, my brother teases me.
I hate it.
I wish
I wish I could go back in time
And play it all again.

*Luke Sims Wilson  (8)*
*Chadlington CE Primary School*

## WHAT'S INSIDE?

There was a world,
A big world,
A big, hot world.

In that big, hot world
There was a continent,
A hot continent,
A hot, steamy continent.

In the hot, steamy continent
There was a country,
A sweltering country,
A sweltering, yellow country.

In the sweltering, yellow country
Was a pyramid,
A dark pyramid,
A dark, smelly pyramid.

In the dark, smelly pyramid
Was a coffin,
A gloomy coffin,
A gloomy, abandoned coffin.

In the gloomy, abandoned coffin
Was a . . . ?

*Tim Allan  (9)*
*Chadlington CE Primary School*

## MY DOG

My dog
Was called George.

He disappeared
And didn't come back.

We never knew where he went.

He disappeared
And didn't come back.

I hated myself.

He disappeared
And didn't come back.

My insides were knots.

He disappeared
And didn't come back.

My insides
were full
of poisonous
gas.

*He*

*Had*

*Gone.*

***Tom Ogden  (9)***
***Chadlington CE Primary School***

## THE PARCEL

In this world there is a war,
A destructive war,
A destructive, murderous war.

In that war there is a hospital,
A death hospital,
A sad, death hospital.

In that hospital there are lots of people,
A group of people,
A group of injured people.

In that group of injured people is one child,
A bleeding child,
A bleeding child near to death.

All because of a bullet.

A bullet from a war,
A destructive war,
A destructive, murderous war . . .

*Anna Phipps  (10)*
*Chadlington CE Primary School*


## MY DAD

My dad feeds the sheep
and puts the food in a heap
he works all day
to get his pay

He gets up from bed
and bumps his head
and falls on the floor
and begins to snore

My dad is so funny
he likes bread and honey
he drinks loads of beer
which sends him all queer

But I love my dad.

*Kelly Cooper (9)*
*Chadlington CE Primary School*


## OLD WOMAN

When I am an old woman
I want to eat raw egg sandwiches
I want my bed full of spiders to crawl up my neck
And in most of my drinks I want a worm.
Every day
I want to play football with the men.
My team would be called Gran United
The best team of the lot.
I want to have grey hair
And wear big high heels on my shoes
And dance madly
And ride on motorbikes
And get drunk in pubs
And smoke fifty fags a day
And play hopscotch in the playground.
I know I shouldn't but
*I don't care at all*
and that's that.

I know I shouldn't get drunk  . . .
I know I shouldn't play football  . . .
I know I shouldn't  . . .

*Kizzie Shepherd (10)*
*Chadlington CE Primary School*

## HORRIBLE AT TIMES

When my sister says, 'Shut up!'
I say, 'No!'
So, she tats.
I call her
Annoying, irritating, horrible at times.
When my sister arranges my room
I wish she was squashed up
In a cocoon.
I call her
Annoying, irritating, horrible at times.
When my sister fiddles with my things
I wish there was a bee
Who would give her a sting.
I call her annoying, irritating, horrible at times.
I take a jumper out of the airing cupboard.
She snatches it.
Sometimes I wish I could hit her.
I call her
Annoying, irritating, horrible at times.

*Rachel Rossiter (11)*
*Chadlington CE Primary School*


## AUTUMN TIME

The trees are dead
The trees are wonkered
The leaves are brown
They tumble down
The conkers drop
To the ground.

*Frank Sheperd (8)*
*Chadlington CE Primary School*

## I'M ANGRY

When I'm angry
It's because
People are teasing me.
What do I do?
Do I just stay there
And put up with them?
Or do I get underneath
The table and make myself *small?*
But then the dogs
Come and lick me
Then I crawl into my room
And punch my pillows
And squash my stress ball.

I
am
so
angry!

*Freddie Magee  (9)*
*Chadlington CE Primary School*


## DOLPHINS

There was a dolphin who lived in the sea.
Her name was Louisa and she always loved me.
We swam and we played in the surf and the waves,
and had great fun in and out of the caves.
We swam and we swam until the sun met the moon,
and darkness fell all too soon.

*Lydia Cherry  (8)*
*Cropredy CE Primary School*

## THE MONKEY

One day I dreamt I was at the zoo
With three monkeys and a kangaroo.
Then I woke up,
I *was* at the zoo
Because I'm a monkey
Just like you.
I sat on my perch
Quite near the church,
I ate a banana
But oh! What a drama.
I got in a spin,
Then dropped the skin,
Along came the vicar
And had a bad slip up
I heard a loud crack,
He was laid on his back
With his hands together
Praying to heaven.

*Emma Walker  (9)*
*Cropredy CE Primary School*


## THE PLUMBER

Our bathroom sink it has a leak,
we called the plumber out last week!
He's so busy, he is not around,
but for the drain we would have drowned!
We made a boat out of our bath
but with all of us in it, it broke in half!
Eventually the plumber came,
but my dad had fixed it so he went again.

*Kate Fallon  (9)*
*Crowmarsh Gifford CE Primary School*

## FOOTBALL CRAZY

F antastic feeling, the team all together.
O n the pitch we stretch our muscles.
O nly one minute to the start of the game.
T ossing a coin in the centre circle.
B oots cleaned and polished, ready for action.
A whistle blows, the game has started.
L ong balls, short balls, volleying and tackling.
L istening to the manager at half-time.

C heering supporters stand on the touch line.
R yan Giggs, I wish you were here.
A lready the game is nearly over.
Z oom, the ball flies in the back of the net.
Y ippee, we've scored a goal.

*Sam Elkins (8)*
*Crowmarsh Gifford CE Primary School*


## FOOTBALL POEM

Football is fun
Playing matches
Scoring goals
Saving them
Football's fun
Getting muddy
Game by game
Cheering crowds
Supporting them
Winning, losing
Football's that
You can't play with a basketball.

*Huw Sadler (9)*
*Crowmarsh Gifford CE Primary School*

## QUESTIONS! QUESTIONS! QUESTIONS!

Is the moon
made of cheese?
Tell me now
please, please.

Is the sun
made of gold?
Is it really
really old?

Is a star
a twinkling pool?
Or is it really
a silver jewel?

Is the sky
held so high
by Atlas
who stands nearby?

For the questions
in my mind,
all the answers
I must find.

*Kaia Parrett  (8)*
*Crowmarsh Gifford CE Primary School*


## MY SENSES

My senses smell the strangest smell
A tortoise simmering in its shell
A snake that's hissing bubbling hot
All in a covered cooking pot.

*Leon Mulcahy  (8)*
*Crowmarsh Gifford CE Primary School*

## WINTER WONDERLAND

Snowflakes falling down and down,
Soft and graceful, not a sound.
Frosty diamonds on the trees,
Sparkling brightly in the breeze.
Children playing in the snow,
Bright red cheeks are all aglow.
Mittened hands and booted feet,
All designed to keep in heat.
Lots of footprints in the snow,
Who they belong to I don't know.
Jack Frost's patterns are all around,
Also icy puddles on the ground.

All in a winter wonderland.

*Thomas Mitchell (8)*
*Crowmarsh Gifford CE Primary School*

## SEASONS

Warm summer sun
sparkling water
glistening lakes clear and cool.
Cold winter wind
frozen brooks
heavy snowfalls.
Light spring breezes
blossoming trees
the sweet scent flows.
Chilly autumn winds
crisp red leaves
lying scattered around.

*Samuel Diserens*
*Crowmarsh Gifford CE Primary School*

## FOOTBALL FOREVER

Football is my favourite game
I play it all day long.
Chelsea are the team I support
they have a special song.

The song is Chelsea, Chelsea,
we sing it at the ground.
We go to Stamford Bridge to watch
them kick the ball around.

My favourite player is Wisey
and Petrescu at the back.
We have a new Italian boss
'cos the last one got the sack.

We might not win the Premiership
but we are in the Coca Cola Cup.
Next year will be even better
'cos Chelsea are on the up and up.

Goals come from the strikers
Hughes, Vialli, Zola and Flo.
I like to go to matches
and shout 'Go Chelsea go.'

Last year we won a trophy
the first for twenty-six years.
It was won the hardest way
with blood and sweat and tears.

I will always support Chelsea
they are the only team for me.
I want to play for them one day
and be the king of Stamford B.

*Luke MacAuley (9)*
*Crowmarsh Gifford CE Primary School*

## BUNNY

My pony is named Bunny,
you may think that's funny
but I think it suits her well.

She is always pleased to see me,
when I go into her stable
I can always tell.

She is a light Palomino
with a soft pretty face.
She likes to trot around
in a wide open space.

She is my very best friend,
our friendship will never end.
She will always stay close to me,
together as we should be.

*Eloise Millett (8)*
*Crowmarsh Gifford CE Primary School*


## IN THE SPRING

The weather's getting warmer,
I love this time of year,
Winter's nearly over,
Summer's nearly here.

In spring the children play outside,
Their parents call, they run inside.

In spring it's time to clear the house,
So you wouldn't even find a mouse!

*Claire Bates (8)*
*Crowmarsh Gifford CE Primary School*

## FROG

I saw a fat frog slipping into a pond
One webbed toe
Then out he jumped
He hopped all over the garden green
He stopped
Stared round
Then carefully he lowered his toe again
He croaked. Disappeared
Remarkable frog.

*Emily Leiber (8)*
*Crowmarsh Gifford CE Primary School*


## THE EVENING SUN

Sun beaming streaks across the wastelands of the African desert.
Hairy camels drink from the warm waters of the waterholes.
Warthogs lie sun soothed.
Evening passes on.
One by one animals crumple into sleep.
The night is drawing in.

*Henry Fletcher (8)*
*Crowmarsh Gifford CE Primary School*


## BLISTERING BICESTER

There was a young man from Bicester
Whose foot came up in a blister
He said 'That's not fair
They always land there
Why can't they land on my sister?'

*Hannah Coates (9)*
*Crowmarsh Gifford CE Primary School*

## HELL

Under ground in the depths of the earth
With larva pools and roaring fire
You come here if you are a killer, thug, cheat or liar
If you continue to be bad and do not heed the warning
You will never see the light of day or even sunrise in the morning.

The devil awaits in all his glory
A smile on his face to retell your story
How you will wish you'd led a better life
But it's too late now, there's no going back
He's got you now and that is that!

*Lauren Beer (9)*
*Crowmarsh Gifford CE Primary School*

## THE BLOW TORCH

A devil's fork, bang, rumble, crackle.
The lightning flashes, the thunder rolls.
Trees turn to ashes, the rain washes hair.
And people hide from rain as it pours from skies.
Crumbling trees fall apart, deafening everyone.
Kaboom goes the lightning - I'm dead.
At least that's how I feel.

The storm's over now, everything fine.
Peace is here at last.
The power is gone, the rain is gone.
And nothing is left but me.
My ears have gone pop, my hair is wet.
But what has happened?
There's nothing to show.

*David Rawcliffe (9)*
*The Dragon School*

# THE ARMY

The men-at-arms marched into battle,
Clanking weapons as they went,
Metal everywhere.
Bowmen twanged their bowstrings as they marched,
Quivers held tight - to fight for a knight.
They live in villages - loyal to a knight.

The knight's clinking armour
Leads the village men, with his bright banner,
To fight the enemy.
'Protect the village' he roars.
The knight errant echoes the call.
The baron's armour glimmers in the moonlight.
He leads the knights on 'In the name of the king'.
Earls of the county lead
With dukes loyal to the king.
The dukes are powerful nobles.
All are loyal to the king.

*Alfred Artley (9)*
*The Dragon School*


# THE TIGER

Tiger in the jungle
Tiger in the night
Creeping up on its prey
Something isn't right.

He's coming really close now
His eyes are wild and frisky
And his stripes become a blur
As he races carrying his beauty.

The prey still hasn't seen him
But I can't do anything
I don't know which side to take
The poor little thing.

He pounced, he got it
Then there becomes a good deed done
When some scampering cubs
Come to feast with their mum!

*Alice Chubb  (9)*
*The Dragon School*


## WHAT FUN IT IS TO BE A SCHOOL KID

What fun it is to be a school kid,
it's cool and fun and great.
But there's awful stuff coming up
lying on my plate!

What fun it is to be a magician,
I make things disappear.
It's really good my audience
stand up and shout and cheer!

What fun it is to be a poet,
I think and write and draw.
I did a poem about a lion
with a *big massive claw!*

What fun it is to be a school kid,
it's cool and fun and great,
(that's because teachers don't use canes anymore  . . .)

*Pow!*

*Me and my big mouth!*

*Jason Davison  (9)*
*The Dragon School*

## EASTER (YUCK)

Five, four, three, two, one
It's the holidays
Time for fun
Time to make a getaway
From this school!
Yuck!

No more nagging teachers
Boring lessons
Hard work
And best of all, no more school dinners
Yuck!

Now we'll be eating . . .
*Chocolate!*
Yes chocolate
Chocolate eggs and rabbits
We'll eat until we're sick
Yuck!

But the trouble with holidays is
. . . Church on Easter morning
You can't see your friends
Sometimes you have nothing to do
. . . and granny's cabbage!
Yuck!

Five, four, three, two, one
End of the holidays
School's begun
Hooray let's make a getaway
From the dreadful holiday and . . .
The chocolate, oh the chocolate
I will never look at chocolate
Horrible chocolate
*Yuck!*

The moral of this poem is: Don't eat too many eggs at Easter.

***Joanna Beaufoy (9)***
***The Dragon School***


## BLIND SPOT

His nose tells him
Where to go,
He chases cats,
But he doesn't know.

His body is covered with black and white spots,
His head is a dither with whether or nots.

A drum to him is a thunderstorm,
A chicken's squawk is an elephant's foghorn,
His only food is breadcrumbs and crusts,
But to him his food is corned beef and husks.

He's a lonely figure,
With nowhere to go,
His only shelter is strong wind and snow,
He's a dog, *but* he's blind.

***Ben Lamb (9)***
***The Dragon School***

## THE EVIL HOOVER

Taking up all things in its path,
Otters and seals rushing down to the water's edge,
Roaring, rushing around, destroying everything,
Never ceasing, travelling round the world,
Always twisting, speeding along,
Do not stand in a tornado's way,
Or it will suck you up and take you away.
Sucking, spinning, completely merciless.

*Alexander Dear  (8)*
*The Dragon School*


## SCHOOL

School begins, being late
I missed assembly. I lost my mate
I pushed Jim over in the corridor
I didn't mean it, I'm sure
At playtime I played bang bang
Somebody played with a gate and went clang clang
Home time comes, everybody runs.

*Charles Williams  (8)*
*The Dragon School*


## THE LEOPARD

Leopard in the night.
Leopard saw her prey.
Leopard crouched.
Leopard pounced.
And got her meal today.

Leopard ran.
Leopard stopped.
Leopard chewed her prey.
Leopard sprang into her bed.
Until another day.

*Kate Womersley  (9)*
*The Dragon School*


## THE CAT-LIKE FOG

Fog is like a cat
Prowling around the unexpecting mouse.

Snow is like a bit of very
Soft sand falling off a cliff onto a beach.

A storm is like a sand storm
Or a wild bore rampaging around.

Hail is like a lot of 1p coins
Thrown into a big pond.

*Max Harper  (9)*
*The Dragon School*


## THE SQUIRREL

The squirrel with its bushy tail,
Hunts for nuts, it starts to hail,
It runs under an empty pail,
The hail ceases, the sun comes out,
And the squirrel carries on its tiring
Task of collecting nuts for the winter.

*Harry Mackarness  (9)*
*The Dragon School*

## THE MIST

The mist, licking its lips at passers-by.
Like a black shadow from the sky.
It climbs up drainpipes, down gutters.
Falling off roofs, going through shutters.
It comes down like a swirling cloud.
Coming, coming to the town.
Going, going down the drain.
Swirls around you but no pain.
Curling around the world like a cat.
Or getting on the world like a hat.

Only one thing can get in locked rooms.
Only one thing ruins tunes.

The mist!

*Bartholomew Quinn (9)*
*The Dragon School*


## MOTHER'S DAY

Today it is Mother's Day, Mother's Day you say?
I wake up from shouts of 'Hip hip hooray'
I get up and dressed, and make her some tea
I bring it upstairs, and she kisses me
I hate Mother's Day, rush around after Mum
While she's just in bed saying 'Ho hum hum hum'
Soon it is lunch, Mum *is* pleased with me
I bring up the lunch and wish it is tea
Mum stays in bed, it comes up to dinner
I carry it up feeling thinner and thinner
At last it's the end of Mother's Day
Now *I'm* feeling hip hip, hip hip hooray.

*Alice Gye (8)*
*The Dragon School*

## THE PANTHER

Black as night,
Alert as day,
Every light,
He sees.

His bright green eyes
Look full of energy,
When he just peacefully lies
Hoping absolutely nothing.

At sunset,
He wanders back to rest
Slowly through the trees,
Not panting, not racing.

*Charlotte Beale  (8)*
*The Dragon School*


## THE THREE KINGS

The three kings on the first Christmas night,
They don't like to admit it, but they had a fight.
Oh what a quarrel it was, under the light
Of that huge star.

And to them it never did occur,
That their gifts, gold, incense and myrrh,
Were lighted by, oh yes they were,
By that huge star.

That fight was all about which gift was the best,
When gold was said he beat his chest.
But then they knew that the best,
Was that huge star.

*Freya Gye  (8)*
*The Dragon School*

## TIGER

The tiger slinks cautiously through the dry, rustling grass
Its big feet pad gently on the hard cracked ground
He spots an eating deer, his prey
The big creature creeps carefully up to the deer
The tiger crouches down ready to pounce
Then . . . he flies gracefully through the air and
Lands on the helpless, innocent deer.
Dinnertime!

*Alice Newell-Hanson  (9)*
*The Dragon School*


## NASTY WEATHER

The storm is like a rhino on a wild charge from heaven.
Its eyes gleam red like lightning and its feet rumble like thunder.
It's as if the gods are angry and have sent a punishment.

The snow is a tide of never ending sea.
It reminds me of a snow rabbit hopping happily through the wood.
It's like being in the middle of nowhere.

*Thomas Brown  (9)*
*The Dragon School*


## A WEATHER POEM

Mist is like a white thorn bush growing and curling around
anything in its way, nothing can kill it, it is invincible,
everything will get lost inside it, when you get lost in mist
you get lost forever.

Cold is like a ghost, you can't see it but you just know it's there.
It can get you and give you frostbite.

*George North  (9)*
*The Dragon School*

## SALLY MINTOPLIN KINTOPLAR MCCREE

Sally Mintoplin Kintoplar McCree,
Of all other things, a gypsy was she.
Jo-Jo O'Major Korajor McMorse,
Of all other things was a gypsy's fine horse.
Ladybird Maraven Kietaven McOak,
Out of everything else was a gypsy's red cloak.

They came to a river, each attempt had been a loss,
And life's greatest problem - that they needed to cross.
Said Ladybird Moraven Kietaven McOak,
'Twist me around so I make a good rope
Then I need someone brave, to valiantly
Take me across and hook me on a tree.'

Said Jo-Jo O'Major Korajor McMorse,
'I can swim, I'm as strong as the heather and gorse,
But first (or else our whole plan will fail)
I need someone deft, to tie the rope to my tail.'

Said Sally Mintoplin Kintoplar McCree
'I weave and tie knots, like all other gypsies.
'I', this rope, can easily tie fast,
Then we can cross o'er this river at last.'

So Sally Mintoplin Kintoplar McCree
Tied the rope to the tail as tight as can be.
And Jo-Jo O'Major Korajor McMorse
Crossed through the waves, a perilous course.
Then Ladybird Moraven Kietaven McOak
Would herself 'round the tree with out even a croak.
The tree is sound, the line is cast,
And they all crossed o'er the river at last.

*Hannah Rickman  (9)*
*The Dragon School*

## LIGHTNING

The lightning is fierce in storms
it comes down in electric flash,
he always wants to come out,
but when the sun comes
he stays in,
but when the sun gets dim,
he nips about and then
he suddenly bursts out,
he does not like it when it's sunny
but when it's dark he hops around
like a mad bunny.
He does not like human beings,
when he sees a good place to strike
he gets to that place really quickly,
it's like he is riding a bike.

*Rory Botros  (9)*
*The Dragon School*


## THE BLACK CAT

The black cat crawls
Around the sofa.
Cat walking.
Hardly waking.
Out in the kitchen.
At night.
Moving
To and fro.
Where can he go?
The black cat sleeps.
Never waking.

*Hermione Waterfield  (8)*
*The Dragon School*

## WHEN WILL I GET A DOG?

When will I get a dog Mum?
I will feed it Pedigree Chum.
Oh when will I get a dog?

When will I get a dog Mum?
If I do I will raise my thumb.
Oh when will I get a dog?

When will I get a dog Mum?
I promise I'll never feed it gum.
Oh when will I get a dog?

When will I get a dog Mum?
I will teach it to come.
Oh when will I get a dog?

When will I get a dog Mum?
I will not feed it rum.
Oh when will I get a dog?

When will I get a dog Mum?
It will not have a big tum.
Oh when will I get a dog?

*Arianna Rees  (9)*
*The Dragon School*


## THE AWFUL NIGHT

Devils rolling their eyes around you,
Aliens spitting and shooting laser guns,
Witches cackling, mumbling nasty spells,
Bulls charging around your bed,
Old women cooking things in cauldrons,
That awful night before school starts!

*Oliver Minton  (8)*
*The Dragon School*

# LOST LEAF

I rustle, I am a green goddess, high up
in the branches. Fluttering, filtering
through high twigs of crisp, crumpled leaves.
Me, sadly in the winter I die,
but, I almost always have a son
or daughter to take my place.
Because now I am a lost fairy,
only a mint leaf, fluttering to
the ground.
I sway, I swish,
I am mustard, I am gold,
slowly my story has been told.
But now a new leaf takes
my place and slowly finds its grace,
while I flinch in the wind,
on the ground, left to die.

*Catherine Pelton  (8)*
*The Dragon School*


## A WINDY NIGHT

Wind curls round the iron railings slowly.
The cold is dark and scary and then the snow
falls onto the railings.
The storm comes in and lights up and bangs
the snow still falling onto everything like sugar.
Then the storm lights up and bangs again, then
it all dies down a bit, but then it starts up again.
It wasn't nice, I did not like it.

*Thomas Ellis  (8)*
*The Dragon School*

## TORNADO

The wind is strong,
The wind is fierce,
It picks up anything in its path,
Whirling round and round,
Ripping tiles off houses,
And spitting them out the top.

The wind howls like a wolf,
It whirls like a whirlpool,
It shouts like thunder,
It sucks up trees as it goes.

The wind is a menace,
The wind plays with leaves,
It swirls off speeding astray,
With its beady eye leading the way.

*George Brown  (9)*
*The Dragon School*


## SHOWING OFF

'I went to the Leaning Tower of Pisa.'
'So what? I went to Gisa.'
'I went to Timbuktu.'
'And I went to Waterloo.'
'I've seen the Mona Lisa.'
'I saw a film about Caesar.'
'Well my dad's a millionaire.'
'Well so am I, so there.'

*Henry Freeland  (8)*
*The Dragon School*

## Roman Candle

R eigning supreme over all fireworks,
O ff they go with a big loud bang!
M en gaze in awe as they go up and down,
A sight to see all over the land!
N ever in the world was there a firework better.

C avaliers marching across the sky,
A mazing to see as they go by!
N ecklaces made of rubies and pearls,
D ancing across, twisting into curls,
L ighting up the boundless sky,
E re they fizzle, ere they die.

*Arjun Kingdon (9)*
*The Dragon School*


## How The Wind Began

The wind began when God breathed out,
The world around Him shook,
Oh that empty round blue thing,
Then God heard the knock at the door,
And left in sudden awe,
And left the wind to play,
That very terrible day,
The wind escaped,
Down to Earth from Heaven,
He whisked through the chimney pots,
And surfed menacingly along the ground,
When men came to inspect the damage,
There was nothing to be found.

*Olly Rowse (9)*
*The Dragon School*

# LEAVES

Leaves settle
and fall, flicker
and wave, sway and sweep,
like a bird descending and
gliding all day. They tumble their
veins like fish bones shrivelled and
delicate, creped and crinkled, shadowed
and silhouetted. They flutter past you
sometimes fast, sometimes slow.
They rustle and whistle, crackle and crumple.
Their colours are beautiful, mustard mingled
with mint and gold, crimson, yellow
and terracotta. When I turn these colours
I fall like a fairy to the ground.

*Henrietta Southby (8)*
*The Dragon School*


# LEAF NEST

In my cosy little nest
The leaves are looking their best
Some are spiky, some are soft
And the old leaves turn into compost
When it rains they feel slimy
Like the pet fish called Whimy
Soon the colours die to copper, ruby, mint and gold
When the new tree grows, all the leaves unfold
How I wish they would come to me in my
Little nest under the cosy, cosy, rustling apple tree.

*Katy Baddeley (8)*
*The Dragon School*

## SNOTTLES

They come in when you're asleep.
They make little squeaking noises.
They try and get into your bed.
They squirm into your covers.
They treat your belongings as their own.
But when the morning comes, they're gone . . .
They will be back.

*Sophie Percival (9)*
*The Dragon School*


## THE WEATHER BATTLE

The thunder booms his war cry,
Lightning rides across the sky;
Swiftly he throws his lances
For the weather's on the pry!
The thunder shouts determinedly,
Tearing the air in two.
Don't go out on a night like this,
Or the victim might be *you!*

*Minoo Dinshaw (9)*
*The Dragon School*


## WINTER POEM

Trees bowing down to the wind,
In the direction of the windmill.
It whooshed and waved.
The windmill went round and round.
After the wind, the storm always comes.

The storm is loud.
It sits and waits for a view of the town;
And then it crashes to the ground . . .
Where people are nice and safe at home.
But the people outside are the mice
to the big cat in the sky.

*Alice Long  (8)*
*The Dragon School*


## MARCH TO WAR

The sound of bugles and of drums.
Boom, toot, boom, toot.
Load the rifles, shoot the guns.
Click, bang, click, bang.
They march by day, they march by night.
Day, night, day, night.
They march, they march, oh how they march.
March to war, march to war.

*Sammy Jay  (9)*
*The Dragon School*


## MONEY

It's the king of the world
!Money!
We worship it, it's powerful
*!Money!*
It fills us with happiness
*!Money!*
(Even though it's just paper)
*!Money!*

*James Henshaw  (8)*
*The Dragon School*

## ROMAN CANDLE

R ising gold sparks
O n up into the air
M agic beauty, go on into the night
A nd when you stop, our heart breaks as the other fireworks go on
N ow I am sad as my happiness is gone.

C alling for more isn't working
A nd I am starting to cry
N ever will I see you until another year goes by
D ead, with no heat, no energy
L ost in the air, my heart is sinking
E ver come back?

*Georgia Booth  (9)*
*The Dragon School*


## A SHADOW OF THE NIGHT

Flimsy frail, white tip tail
delicately dappled, swift silent.
Inquisitive, gentle, shy, defiant
Autumn enemies deter.
Prancing prince, dancing deity.
Warm tongue, soft muzzle.
Lifts head, alert intent
and then a leap,
a memory to keep.
Blown in the wind a soft, silk, sleek rag.
The midnight stag.

*Jenny Bulstrode  (9)*
*The Dragon School*

## THE NIGHTMARE

I had a nightmare last night
It was about a monster
I really didn't like it
There I was out camping
Monster came out from a bush
Trampled all over our food
Made massive footprints in the ground
I ran like the wind
Monster ran right behind me
*Idea*
I jumped behind a bush
Monster kept going
I got some thin string
Tied it to a tree
Monster came back
Tripped over the string
And *splash* into the lake
End of monster.

*Matthew Starie  (7)*
*Edward Feild School*

## BOYS

Boys are ugly, boys are mad.
Boys play football, they are sad.
Boys are thick like a custard stick.
Girls are cute like a lollipop stick.

But the best in the world
Are girls
*Super girls.*

*Natasha Simmons  (9)*
*Edward Feild School*

## WILD FOOTBALL

Wild football in town,
On the grass,
Wild football
Newcastle against Man United
Wild football
Alan kicks the ball in the sky
Wild football
It's in the net!
Wild football
Score is one-one
Who won?
Wild football
Newcastle wins, Man United loses
The crowd cheered,
Wild football
The crowd shout out loud in the sun
Wild football
All the players have a bottle of champagne,
Man United didn't win, so they don't get one.

*Wild football!*
*Wild football!*
*Wild football!*

*Jordan Hussain  (9)*
*Edward Feild School*


## MONSTER

It's got goggle eyes and a big fat head,
and always snores when he is in bed.
His voice is so growly, so loud and so sore.
It sounds like my brother,
but I can't tell you any more.

Growl, growl he goes up to bed,
but oh no, he hasn't been feed.
Growl, growl, he's growling louder,
he's got so angry, he's turned into powder.

*Claire England  (9)*
*Edward Feild School*


## A Daisy

I saw a daisy
Yellow and white
With petals that glistened
In the light
It had a green stem
With light green leaves
And it made me think of a
Sparkling fish glittering in the dark blue sea
I thought that daisy was so, so beautiful.

*Nicola Blake  (8)*
*Edward Feild School*


## My Baby Brother

My baby brother John,
Cries all day whether he's having his nappy changed
or going out to play.
He's only got six teeth, two at the top and four at the bottom.
He's got hazelnut coloured eyes that glisten in the sun.
He has bright blond hair that sparkles everywhere.
He's got pale red lips and a very cheeky grin!

*Emma Crockett  (8)*
*Edward Feild School*

## My Family

There's my brother Matthew
who supports *Man United*
he's a very big fan.

Then there's Mum
who is
helpful
kind and caring.

Dad has always got his head under a car
fixing it
his job is driving a van.

Our dog Max is always ill
and he's costing us a lot of money.

And then there's me
well I don't really know what to say
but I am quite sure that if you ask any of my family
they will say something nice about me!
(I hope.)

*Rebecca Simmonds  (9)*
*Edward Feild School*

## Poem

I had a dog
He chewed on a log
He ran like a rocket
And jumped like a frog

I had a cat
That crawled like a rat
He ran across the kitchen
And jumped on the mat

I had a bird
It could only say one word
One day it escaped
And so never was heard.

*Matthew Smith  (8)*
*Edward Feild School*


## THE JUNGLE LION

I bought my sister
a lion mask
On the way home
I met a lion
I looked at the lion
I screamed
It was my sister
wearing her lion mask.

*Chantelle Rowlands  (8)*
*Edward Feild School*


## GRANNY

Granny is special, special, special.
She lets me play with any toys.

Granny is special, special, special.
She reads me bedtime stories.

Granny is special, special, special.
She gives me sweets - yummy.

*Heather Williams  (7)*
*Edward Feild School*

## MY MUM'S A WITCH

My mum's a witch
A very nice witch.
She does all the work
As quick as a flash.
She does all the work
As quick as that.

I love my mum
She's really cool.
What she does
Is very good.
She just zaps me
To the school and
There I am.
Hey presto.
My mum's a witch
A very nice witch.

*Rahim Hakimi  (8)*
*Edward Feild School*


## GRANNY

I love my granny
And she loves me.

I love my granny
She is special to me.

I visit my granny
She gives me sweets.

I love my granny
And she loves me.

*Kristy Collins  (8)*
*Edward Feild School*

## MY BABY NIECE

She cries and cries
She feeds herself
Messy, messy, messy
Food in her hair
Food everywhere
She cries and cries
She eats her shoes
She cries and cries
But never goes to sleep
Cry, cry, cry
Put her in your arms
Now she is fast asleep.

*Katie Jackson  (8)*
*Edward Feild School*


## WIND

Wind wind
Scary wind
Whistling through the keyhole.
Wind wind
Scary wind
Keeping me awake.
Wind wind
Scary wind
Blowing me away.
Wind wind
Scary wind
Whistling through the keyhole.

*Charlotte McInerney  (8)*
*Edward Feild School*

## IN MY BED

Lying in my bed,
I look through my curtains I see,
a kind of ghost.
Getting scared.
My brother is snoring.
Still in my bed
hear a crack under the bed.
I got out of my bed
I open the curtains
It's my sister.
Look under the bed
It's my dad.
Go over to my brother's bed
I see my talk boy, it's got me snoring on it.

My brother goes  . . .  *boo.*

*Mark White  (9)*
*Edward Feild School*


## HIDING IN MY BEDROOM

Come come
Find me
Will I starve
Hiding in my bedroom
Without any food
Find me
Help me
*Mum!*
Find me
*Quick.*

*Hannah Tripkovic  (8)*
*Edward Feild School*

## BREATHLESS

I am trying to speed up.
I cannot fail.
Let me get up.
My heart won't fail.
I'm speeding up.
Resting point here.
Got to stop.
Got to breathe.
Let me stop.
I'm stopping here.
I've stopped here.
I'm trying to speed up.
I cannot fail.
My heart won't fail.
It's over now.
I'm at the top.

*Laura Thompson (9)*
*Edward Feild School*


## THE PLANT IN THE WINDOW

The plant in the window does nothing but sit there
all day long.
It feels smooth and it's very shiny from the sun.
The plant in the window has red and pink pointed leaves.
When the leaves go bad they curl up.
The plant in the window is very large and has tall leaves
and a big stem.
The plant in the window has lots of colours - red, yellow,
brown, pink and green.

*Shelley Litten (10)*
*Edward Feild School*

## There's a Demon Under My Bed

*'Muuuum, there's a demon under my bed.'*
'What nonsense just go to bed.'

*Muuuum, there's a demon under my bed.'*
'If I hear one more noise out of you
there'll be no pocket money for a year.'

*'Muuuum, there's a demon under my bed.'*
'Right that's it
I'm c o m i n g up the stairs . . .

So, where is that demon . . . ?'
*'Under my bed . . . '*

So she looked under my bed
It was my annoying brother Ian
Hiding
But he wasn't laughing because
he had no pocket money for a year.

***Simon Marris (8)***
***Edward Feild School***


## Verse For My Dad

From me to you at Christmas time,
Drink loads of beer,
And bottles of wine!

From me to you with Christmas cheer,
My message to you is very clear.

From me to you with Christmas snore,
Make sure you don't end up on the floor!

***Dan Sanders (10)***
***Edward Feild School***

## Hide And Seek

Going up a tree
Counting one, two, three
Ready or not here I come
She looks and she looks
But she doesn't find me.

Hiding in the garden
Going in the shed
Counting one, two, three
Ready or not here I come
She looks and she looks
There she comes. I run.

*Jodie Atkin  (8)*
*Edward Feild School*


## Boys

Boys get out of their chairs
Tell their teachers 'It's not fair'
Some boys are really tall
But they all like football.

Boys get dirty
Boys get wet
Boys have spiders for their pets.

Boys hate kissing Auntie Jean
Boys try being like Mr Bean
With boys it's not great or cool
To sit with dolly on a stool.

*Georgina Stillgoe  (8)*
*Edward Feild School*

## GIRLS ARE DIFFERENT

Girls play with their dollies
giggle a lot
cry for nothing
and skip on the spot
dress up like their mum
love Boyzone
speak very softly
and stick out their tongues
tell tales all the time
suck their hair
read pony books
and whisper in pairs

All I want to say
to girls and all
that the greatest thing
around is
*football!*

***Richard Weston  (9)***
***Edward Feild School***


## THE DANCING DOLPHINS

I heard the dolphins one night
I could hear them singing
and swaying in the waves
I heard them say
'We are the dancing dolphins'
Then I saw them disappear
into the waves.

***Jessica Strong  (9)***
***Edward Feild School***

## DAD AND MUM

One day
I was talking to Dad
Dad said
'I was never bad.'
But if Dad rubbed
*D* out and put a *b*
Dad would be bad.
So I'm not bad
Dad is!

And after that
Mum asks me
'What is 800 x 62?'
I said 'Well' I said 'I don't know I'm only 2.'
Because rub *M* out and put *d*
Mum would be dum
So I'm not dum
Mum is!

*Peter Salcombe  (9)*
*Edward Feild School*


## SHARK

His teeth are daggers
Sharp and strong,

His body is a rain-cloud
Heavy and long,

The shark is a cheetah
King of the sea.

*Laura Ferris  (9)*
*Edward Feild School*

## I WONDER WHY

I wonder
Why the sky is blue?
I wonder why
A lie is a lie?
So why
Is a greenhouse green?
I wonder
Why sea is blue?
As I sit
I wonder why
It feels like
Winter when
Spring is nigh?
As these wonders
Come to me,
I wonder why?
I wonder!

*Mary-Hannah Bailey  (8)*
*Edward Feild School*


## MY STAR

My star is my star forever
because
My star is as bright as the midday sun
My star is a floating yacht
across a calm sea
My star is as gentle as a floating feather
because
My star is my star forever.

*Robert Sheldon  (9)*
*Edward Feild School*

## WHY DO GROWN-UPS SAY?

Why do grown-ups say
'Go to bed'
When it's only 8 o'clock?

Why do grown-ups say
'We're going shopping'
When you're just about to watch your favourite TV programme?

Why do grown-ups say
'Wake up'
When it's 6 o'clock in the morning?

Why do grown-ups say
'Tidy your room'
When it's your room and you should be allowed to keep it
how you like?

*Why do grown-ups say?*

**Laura Murray (9)**
**Edward Feild School**


## PLAYING FOOTBALL

We are winning
Ball on the floor
Ball in the air
Yes, a goal!
Football in the air
Football in the goal
Yes, football over the line
Throw in!

**Louie Bunn (7)**
**Edward Feild School**

## THE TORTOISE

Slowly plodding along the cold river bank.
Hard, scaly shell.
Big footsteps.
Cutting through the long grass.
Step by step.
Goes a little further.
Then a shadow appears
on a nearby rock.
Scares tortoise
and he hides in his shell.
Then tortoise goes down
to the river bank
and swims away.

*Alison Howes  (10)*
*Edward Feild School*


## BLUE SKY

Lovely morning
Blue sky, no clouds
Quick up
Get dressed
Fill paddling pool
Get towels
Get sunshade
Swimsuit on
Glasses on
And  . . .
*It starts to rain.*

*Sophie Davies  (7)*
*Edward Feild School*

## THE CAT'S DAY

The cat wakes up,
spreads his paws.
Moves about,
spreads his claws.

Stands up,
has a yawn.
Moves about,
and greets the dawn.

Goes in the garden,
smells the flowers.
Moves about,
feels the day's great powers.

Goes inside,
smells the food.
Moves about,
feels the mood.

Goes to the lounge,
nice and comfy.
Moves about,
its name is Fluffy.

Goes to bed,
wants some cream.
Moves about,
has a dream.

*Yasamin Kazemi  (10)*
*Edward Feild School*

## THE SHARK'S TOOTH

A shark's teeth, where do they find them,
in his mouth or right inside him?
Did he eat a baby shark,
or did he chip it in the park?
Did he chip it on a rock,
or did he chip it whilst in the clock?
Did they kill him and take it out,
or did they take them while he was out?

*Carl Matthew Brooks  (9)*
*Edward Feild School*


## SPAGHETTI

Spaghetti, spaghetti
You are wonderful stuff,
I love you spaghetti,
I can't get enough.
With sauce on the top
And cheese sprinkled on,
Spaghetti, spaghetti
You are the best.

*Samantha Barker  (8)*
*Edward Feild School*


## FRUIT TREES

In the spring they grow their leaves and have pretty blossom.
In the summer the fruit comes ripe like apples and plums.
In the autumn they go yellowy-red.
In the winter they look like twigs.

*Tiffany Fisher  (8)*
*Edward Feild School*

## MY TEDDY

My old bear is really smelly.
His fur is fading now.
But he's still my bear.
My treasure, my one, my only.
He was my first toy and now the best.
My first old bear with velvet paws.
The sad and sorry smile.
A bear with the only eye.
And a nose that's falling off.
He is old and tatty
but he's still the only thing
that brings out all my pleasure!

*Hannah Payne  (10)*
*Edward Feild School*


## MY FAMILY

My dad is a solicitor,
he has us as a visitor.
Whenever he's not working,
he's playing football!
My mum is always working.
On her good day,
she could work for the King!
My brother's rather dotty,
and when he's not being an idiot,
he's driving me potty!

And that's my family!

*Sean Geaney  (8)*
*Edward Feild School*

## THE ROCKET

5 ... 4 ... 3 ... 2 ... 1 ...
The rocket blasts off
It goes through the sky like a torpedo
It flies through space like a Formula 1 car
It's as noisy as Concorde
It's as noisy as a goods train
It's as fast as lightning
It moves like a dragster racing car
It floats like a balloon when the engines turn off
It lands on the planet Z!

*Shaun Stevenson (9)*
*Edward Feild School*


## NIGHT

In the dark
came night
In the night
came light
In the light
was the sun.

*Catherine Grain (7)*
*Edward Feild School*


## THE ELEPHANT

The elephant has feet as big as a car,
ears as big as a parachute
and skin as rough as rusty nails.

The elephant has a trunk as long as an old giraffe's neck,
legs as wide as an old oak tree
and a tail as short as a baby's leg.

The elephant has eyes as small as beads,
their skin is the colour of the clouds on a rainy day
and it is as heavy as 10 tons of bricks.

*Amy Jackson  (10)*
*Edward Feild School*

## UMBRELLA PLANT

Big umbrella plant covering my head.
With thick smooth leaves.
Thick smooth stem.
With healthy leaves reaching out.
But then bedtime.
It creeps over me at night.
I think it's a spider and I scream.
Ahhh!
With fear I wake up.
It wasn't a spider.
It was my plant.

*Kimberley Nash  (9)*
*Edward Feild School*

## THE WIND

Wind going whooshing past.
I am trying to go against the wind.
Now I am flying in the air.
Down I go, the wind has stopped.

*Calum Surrage  (7)*
*Edward Feild School*

## MY HAND

Soft,
Smooth,
Bumpy,
Swirling waves,
A firework bang,
Crinkly,
Strong,
Swirly,
An explosion,
A relaxing feeling,
Stiff,
Stretchy,
Wrinkled,
Stones splashing in water,
Ivy,
Maze.

*Daniel Langlay-Smith (11)*
*Faringdon Junior School*

## THE PLAYGROUND

Children rush down the stairs
Try to be out first
Snatch the footballs
Kick 'em around -
It's playtime.

Slowly the playground fills right up
Footballs smash the windows!
Teachers shouting
Boys are fighting -
It's playtime.

A game of round the wall goes on
They're jumping over rocks
Bash into people with skateboards
Little children running around -
It's playtime.

And then the bell begins to ring
They gobble down the last of their crisps
The rush to get in
The screeching up the stairs
That's playtime.

*Kathryn Whiffen  (11)*
*Faringdon Junior School*


## MY HAND IS:

My hand is:
Rows of lots of houses,
Purple and pink spots,
Green and blue dots,
Cuts and bruises,
Bumped up knuckles,
Veins like rivers flowing through a forest,
It has a woodpecker click,
And an alligator snap,
A dripping tap finger clap,
Shimmery of wind when rubbed together,
Smells of plasticine from yesterday's experiment,
A smell of syrupy porridge from this morning's breakfast,
And of course *me,*
They are sticky and hot,
Bumpy and rough,
And they are my hands.

*Sammy Allen  (10)*
*Faringdon Junior School*

## CLEANING

Cleaning can be pleasant
With all the lovely smells
Like beeswax, Brasso, Zebo
Which smell so lovely and sweet
You always feel cold
And sometimes feel old
Some noises can be chilling
Some noises can be willing
To do it again.
Some noises sound like a train
Rushing down an alley
Like a rushing rally.

*Ben Jones  (10)*
*Faringdon Junior School*


## THOSE OLD VICTORIANS

Old fashioned clothing,
Happy but cold,
Warm splashing water,
Very creamy soap,
The smell of beeswax,
The stench of Brasso,
The soft feel of rag rugs,
The gleam of polished brass,
Those old Victorians,
Haven't got a clue,
Do everything the hard way,
Don't know what to do.

*Charlie Green  (9)*
*Faringdon Junior School*

## A Day As A Victorian

A day as a Victorian,
is very tiring
but don't give up
keep trying.

In a washroom
mix the Sunlight soap,
but you may
not be able to cope.

There's a lot of washing,
in the big tub,
add the water then the soap,
then you just have to rub.

It's time to hang the
washing out to dry
peg it up well, oops
there's dirt on the leg.

*Robert Harte  (10)*
*Faringdon Junior School*


## My Hands

My hand smells of my breakfast, chocolate on
toast and me and my house.
It reminds me of scars and cracks in an egg.
Lots of lines, lots of dots and a couple of red spots.
Sticky and hot.
Some bits smooth and some bits rough.
Bumpy knuckles and a tapping sound.
Draught of wind and a crocodile  . . .  *snap!*

*Alex Oliver  (10)*
*Faringdon Junior School*

## MY HAND

Lots of cracks in my hand
Looks like ice in the winter
Feels like it too
When I pull it, it sounds like a window smashing.
My hands feel just like a big back road.

*Ben Ledbury (11)*
*Faringdon Junior School*


## MY HAND

My hand is
short and has short palms
It smells of rubber
I have blue veins
When you rub my hands they are smooth
My nails are pink with white on them
and when I click my fingers, it makes a noise.

*Kate Bradbury (9)*
*Faringdon Junior School*


## GAMES

Children are running,
Some children are crying,
Some children are happy,
Children are squealing in the playground,
I am alone.

*Steven Hall (9)*
*Faringdon Junior School*

## MY HAND

My hand is:
A baseball if it was round
A bit like a maze
Wrinkly
An explosion
A giant bang
Stones splashing in water
Water splashed on the ground
Calm
Ticklish
Bumpy.

*Simon Ho (11)*
*Faringdon Junior School*


## UNTITLED
The playground is:-
running like lions,
moving as slow as the sun,
screaming like cats,
talking like mum,
children on their own,
lonely like flamingos,
as sad as the goal post,
looking as sad as snow,
salt and vinegar crisp smells,
children standing in the corner,
the smell of people's hair.

*Jennifer Arlott (10)*
*Faringdon Junior School*

## THE PLAYGROUND

The playground is like:
The crunching of crisps like leaves,
Cries of happiness and anger,
Children on rollerblades darting about,
Watch out! Too late, children screaming,
They've been hit,
Skipping ropes tapping the ground,
These are the noises of the playground.

*Alison Jerome  (10)*
*Faringdon Junior School*


## THE BLACKBOARD

I have a blackboard in my class,
And it's black as black can be,
Until my teacher writes on it and says,
'Oh stop writing on me.'

*Kim Massey  (10)*
*Faringdon Junior School*


## HORIZON

Golden beam and orange reflection
    shining on the silver sea
On the beach the crabs are having tea
    The clams are singing
I sit on the sand and watch the sunset
    while the starfish do cartwheels
I wish I didn't have to leave this
    lovely day.

*Sophie Durham  (8)*
*Ferndale School*

## A BIRD

In the country,
In the city,
I fly with scraps of bread.

In the shop I steal some buns,
To feed my little ones.

In the winter 'more twigs please!'
Cold and wet, no more scraps
My wings can barely flap.

But spring so soon,
It's not even noon,
There's scraps once again
And lots of buns so I
Can feed my little ones.

*Katy McLaven  (8)*
*Ferndale School*


## ALIENS

Aliens are big and slimy and ugly
Some have forty eyes and
others have a hundred legs.

One alien had four hundred eyebrows!
Some have veins all through their legs.

Some have huge spaceships that
fly in the sky.

Around every corner you
will find
Aliens!

*Hamish Muir  (9)*
*Ferndale School*

## UNDER THE SEA

Under the sea
On the sandy bed
Lies a coral palace
Pink and white

Under the sea
In the coral palace
In and out go the fish
Pink and white

Under the sea
Outside the coral
Are lots of pretty flowers
Pink and white

Under the sea
On the sandy bed
Many, many things are  . . .
Pink and white!

*Katherine Prior  (9)*
*Ferndale School*


## THE ROLLER-COASTERS

The roller-coaster goes up and down
The roller-coaster goes day and night
People are queuing every day
Gosh, it must be bad.

Roller-coasters are big
Roller-coasters are small
Roller-coasters everywhere
Roller-coasters are a scream!

People are screaming
Roller-coasters never stop
They go upside down
But the roller-coaster is a
Scream . . .

*Vishal Madhani (8)*
*Ferndale School*


## SCARED

I am scared,
I can't get this off my mind,
This is something I cannot find.

There is something scary in my house,
For heaven's sake it's only a mouse.

No it isn't,
Is it the cradle?
Rocking to and fro, to and fro.

Impossible! It's my mum
She is dumb.

Walking around in the night,
Switching on all the lights,
Going to the kitchen.

It could not be.

It must be the *giant* legless flea!
*No! No!*
What is it? It's rocking me!
*Help!*
I wake up, I'm safe in my bed.

*Kate Harrison (8)*
*Ferndale School*

## TEDDY BEARS

Teddy bears, teddy bears,
Big or small,
Medium or tiny,
Teddy bears sweet.

I love teddy bears,
*Floral Bear,*
*Message Bear,*
Teddy bears sweet.

I adore them,
They are cuddly,
Can you guess who I mean?
*Forever Friends!*

**Amy Daniels (8)**
**Ferndale School**


## OUR ANIMALS

I hate our turkeys
They peck me to death
They make me mad
I hate, I hate, I hate our *turkeys*

I hate our chicks
They scratch my hand
They make me cross
I hate, I hate, I hate our *chicks*

I hate our pony
It stands on my feet
It makes me mad
I hate, I hate, I hate our *pony.*

**Philippa Burr (9)**
**Ferndale School**

## FOOD

Delicious, delightful
Fun to eat
Whether it's pudding or whether it's meat.

Curry and chilli
are very hot
Pasta and pizza
I like a lot.

Heavenly pudding
And chocolate sauce
Are a wonderful pudding
*Course!*

Biscuits and cheese
Stilton and Brie
Lovely food
all for me!

*Mary Hawken  (8)*
*Ferndale School*


## LAMBS

Skipping, skipping around
Lambs, lambs everywhere
Hopping, hopping in the fields
Baa, baa they say
Cuddling, cuddling them
Dark, dark it is
They are afraid
Owls, owls are singing
Lambs, lambs in the fields.

*Emma Cox  (9)*
*Ferndale School*

## TEACHERS

Why are teachers so bossy?
They shout like thunder.
The door slams when they leave the room
Like lightning attacking a tree.
Oh why, oh why are they so bossy?

If you don't tuck your chair in,
Bong you go straight down to the headmaster.
Then the headmaster goes blue
And pumps up like a balloon.
Oh why, oh why are they so bossy?

I don't understand why you can
Scream your head off in break
And then inside
Silent as some mice.
Oh why, oh why are they so bossy?

*Suzanna Carter  (9)*
*Ferndale School*

## A WINTER'S NIGHT

Winter is here
The sky is dark
Rain might come
Today at the park.

People walk briskly
Upon their way
Umbrellas are carried
All bright and gay.

The flowers aren't out
No one is looking
They all rush by
Back to their cooking.

Into their houses
Then shut the door
Turn on the light
They are no more.

*Matthew Brooks  (9)*
*Ferndale School*


## THE FOUR SEASONS

Spring is great!
The daffodils!
Baby animals are being born!
It's new life.

Summer is great!
The hot, hot sun!
We have the holidays!
It's so sunny.

Autumn is great!
The colourful trees!
The apples on the apple tree!
It's full of colour.

Winter is great!
The cold, cold snow!
Jack Frost is about
It's the end of the year!

*Elizabeth Holdsworth  (9)*
*Ferndale School*

## SCHOOL TIME

The bell has gone,
And I walk out,
I run and jump and leap about,
I talk to my friends and play a game,
I ask the new people what's your name?
They answer me: my name's Melanie,
                    my name's Roy,
One's a girl, one's a boy.

The bell has gone,
I'm in my line,
I've got new friends,
And I feel fine.

*Emma J M L Thompson  (8)*
*Ferndale School*


## KINGS AND QUEENS OF LONG AGO

History is fun
Kings and queens of long ago
Dead in the time trail
Kings and queens of long ago
Once again make their show
Kings and queens of long ago
Henry the seventh, Henry the eighth, Edward the sixth
Kings and queens of long ago
Queen Jane, Queen Mary, Queen Elizabeth
All dead in the
                    *Time trail.*

*Hazel Luck  (8)*
*Ferndale School*

## ALIENS

Aliens are green,
They like pizza and chips.
They go around in flying saucers,
Flying in the sky.
They have no legs.
They're like snails,
Except they don't leave a slimy trail.
They have five eyes and no hair.
Some people say they've seen them.
They call them UFOs.

*Jack Duffy (8)*
*Ferndale School*


## THE FAST FISH

As I follow a very fast fish
It seems to me like a lovely dish
It swims under a waterfall
Then somehow to a swimming pool
Down a river
It seems to shiver!
Into the sea
It looks very happy
He got caught in a net
On your marks get set!
He jumped as high as he could into the sea
Then found himself following a bee
He swam round a whale
Until he got pale
Now the fish is dead
At the bottom of the seabed.

*Miranda Scott (9)*
*Freeland CE Primary School*

## MY FISH POND

My pond is full with lots of fish
I'm sure they'll make a tasty dish.

Imagine a herring or a cat
Eating my fish, how about that?

I bet they wouldn't
They know they shouldn't.

I'll put some bars over my pond
Then they won't be all that fond.

I don't think they would do much harm
To my little pond on the farm.

Imagine my fish in the sea
Swimming happily, strong and free.

But instead of cats with claws
There are big fish with big jaws.

One day fishes I promise you will be
Swimming happily under the sea.

*Hannah McNeil (8)*
*Freeland CE Primary School*


## RAIN AND PUDDLES

Drip, drop down comes the rain.
Drip, drop, drip, drop here it comes again.
It runs down the gutter.
Slips down the roof.
Splashes on the floor.
I hope it won't rain any more.

*Jennifer Collett (8)*
*Freeland CE Primary School*

## THE WICKED SEA OWNERS

Rain falls down in little trickles
Lands in rivers and makes ripples.

Underneath all this water
Is the wicked queen's daughter.

Her and her magic spells
Can turn 3 fishes into bells.

She lives in water caves with her mother
They hide the treasure from the queen's brother.

They are very rich with money
How they hide it, is quite funny.

Then one day they both died
So all the fish are in their pride.

*Tamsin Haigh  (8)*
*Freeland CE Primary School*

## WATERFALLS

Waterfalls fall from above
Waterfalls come very rough
Waterfalls play so tough
Waterfalls are so high
Waterfalls are so tall
Waterfalls go at the speed of light
Waterfalls rush, rush, rush.

*Josh Mutlow  (8)*
*Freeland CE Primary School*

## THE CORAL REEF

Swimming in the coral reef
Funny coloured fish beyond your belief.
Plants and shipwrecks rotting away
Every night and every day.
Stripy and spotty fish swimming about,
Trying to catch food without a doubt.
Plain and prickly, blown up fish,
Swimming about making the water swish.
Funny, wobbly, multicoloured plants,
Swaying about as the sea chants.
Exploring the old ship,
Let's go in for a dip.
Old seats and cutlery,
In this ship that once sailed to sea.
Now in the cabins, a soft bed,
People once laid there, now they're dead.
Out into the fresh sea,
Sharks and octopus fill my tummy.
Now I explore some little caves,
Under the plants there are fish graves.
Winding rock corridors,
Full of mini Minitors.
Open mouthed fish,
Catching a family dish.
Now the sea has stopped in motion,
Now I must leave the ocean.
Back on my boat sailing in my villa,
Maybe there is a sea killer.

*Darius Hodaei (9)*
*Freeland CE Primary School*

## WATERFALL

Waterfall splashing down
rushing into river town.
Underwater fishes swim
diving to the water's rim.

Behind the fall there is a cave
where groups of bats rave.
Dripping water is its slave
waiting for a giant wave.

The water runs down stream
some of them are quite mean.
All of them supreme
their lovely scales shiny cream.

Getting very near the sea
then of course they see me.
I am the water fairy
my water name is Mary.

I control the waters nerves
and steer it round where there are curves.
The currents and torrents are all mine
standing straight in a big long line.

*Beth Hewitt (8)*
*Freeland CE Primary School*

## SUNDAY AFTERNOON

I am most terribly bored,
As the rain goes pat on my door.

I look outside and see the rain,
The rain looks back at me again.

Oh how the rain can be a pain,
I don't know but it's back again.

I hear the raindrops on my roof,
Just like some of the horses' hooves.

*Oh rain please go away!*

**Catherine Hall (8)**
**Freeland CE Primary School**


## GOLDFISH

Splish, splash
Goes the goldfish swimming in his bowl.
Splish, splash
Goes the goldfish playing with his ball.
Bubble, bubble
Goes the goldfish hiding in his bowl.
Bubble, bubble
Goes the goldfish sleeping in his bowl.
Zzzz!

**Paul Jacobs (8)**
**Freeland CE Primary School**

## River Through The Ages

First three verses about the young river.
It's cold on the mountain and I shiver.

What is this? A source (a lake)
water from here this stream does take.

What is this? A little stream
the sun shines and makes it gleam.

There's waterfalls way up here
where snow lies all the year.

The middle age comes at last
now the river's not flowing so fast.

What is this? A bend in the river.
The water's cold and it makes me shiver.

The channel gets wider, deeper too
don't spoil the river, you won't will you?

Now we see the old age nigh
this is the last stage so say goodbye.

What is this? A big muddy delta
the water no longer flows helter-skelter.

Now we're at the open sea
so the river is very happy.

*Lucy McGregor (8)*
*Freeland CE Primary School*

## MY BLACK PUPPY

I have a black puppy
Jasmin's her name
And of course she
Thinks everything's a game
She chews daddy's jumper
She digs great big holes
The garden looks like
We've got lots and lots of moles
When she sees her bone
She jumps up and down
She gets so excited
I can't calm her down
She has puppy food for breakfast
And hot milk for her tea
When she has finished
I tickle her tummy
And stroke her head
We lie there together
And both have a nap.

*Woof, Woof.*

**Laura Watts  (9)**
**Great Milton CE Primary School**


## SPACE

The moon is big and round, big holes in the ground.
Like a giant ball of cheese, floating around.

The sun is a big ball of fire in space,
the planets spinning round and round.
Everything moving in cold black space.
Even though the planetoid goes round and round in
deep black space.

Stars are big and small, sometimes you can't see them at all,
they twinkle and glow at night,
and they guide you through the night.

In space you cannot breathe at all,
you would float in the cold.
Watching comets zooming by,
making patterns as they fly.

*Adam Buck (9)*
*Great Milton CE Primary School*


## OUR HOLIDAY ON THE MOON!

We went to the moon
It's fun there
You bounce up and down
Do as you dare!

Ride in a buggy
Fast as you can
'Watch out' a crater
Close man!

I drove the rocket
Mum got scared
Dad then said 'He did the dare!'

Then I decided to go down a crater
When I was there I saw an alligator!

That was about it
Our holiday on the moon
Hope to go back very soon!

*Simon Toms (8)*
*Great Milton CE Primary School*

## A BIG MISTAKE

A dragon called George
Once went to a school called
The Fat Dragon.
George entered a competition
For poetry.
He cheated though,
He copied his friend,
So,
He didn't get the prize.
He was so angry that his scales
Turned red, his mouth blew fire.
He even threw a wobbly.
He didn't get the gold or silver,
He didn't get the jewels.
He learnt that it wasn't wise to cheat
Because you don't get the prize.

*James Enser  (8)*
*Great Milton CE Primary School*

## GARDEN

Creatures like spiders munch at the plants,
But specially chew on the mint.
Climb up the creeper, eat up the dill,
Then sleep on the window-sill.
Sometimes I can see them from inside,
And that just really gets me.
But where I feel I cannot win
Is when I see them coming in!

*Simon Taylor  (9)*
*Great Milton CE Primary School*

## A CRAB CALLED CRABBY

Pinch! Ouch!
That's my toe!
You naughty little so and so!
That's Crabby,
The crab,
He's always doing that,
He makes me so mad,
He even had the cheek,
To pinch my favourite cat!
The only thing he's scared of,
*Eek!*
Is my leftover luncheon meat!
Now don't laugh,
It's not a joke!
He was once so scared,
He clawed my throat!
Here's a scar to prove it,
Look!
So there's no need to think,
I've been reading a book.
That's how dangerous crabs can be,
I think it was right to put him back in the sea!

*Laura Robinson  (9)*
*Great Milton CE Primary School*

## BLACK'S THIS

Gloomy days
Gloomy nights
Gloomy day and night.
Fire needs coal
Just like we need light.
Black spiders
Crawling out
Of the bath
Biting everybody
As they go past
*Ugh!*

*Jenny Flowers  (7)*
*Great Milton CE Primary School*

## MUM'S TUM

My mum has quite a big tum,
But she's been on a diet for years!
'Maybe I'll start tomorrow or next week,'
'I'll just have this chocolate
Then I'll diet'
'No, wait,
I can't diet today because it's, it's,
Well it's Chocolate Day'
Now, my mum says,
We all have to go on a diet because
My mum can't lose weight.

*Fabienne Morgan  (9)*
*Great Milton CE Primary School*

## THE DAY AT MARS

One day we went to Mars,
For a holiday year,
It was fun, you could make the aliens disappear.
Our spaceship broke down, we called the AA.
But they just said 'Go away.'
We fixed our spaceship, it took a day,
Then all the spare parts were sucked away!
We went crater-hopping, it was fun,
We did it while our spaceship re-charged by the sun.
We had to go back to Earth,
Our mum was going to have a birth.
We can come again next year.
See you then!

*Matthew Winyard (9)*
*Great Milton CE Primary School*


## SINDY DOG

Sindy dog sleeps anywhere
Like a cat.
She has shining eyes
Like diamonds in the sky.
A shining nose
Like fish skin scales.
Lovely, silky fur,
Claws like a big bear.
Sindy never misses an opportunity
*To* go out of an open door.
*'Get the cats Sindy'*
　'Good girl.'

*Aaron Johns (8)*
*Great Milton CE Primary School*

# I AM A ...

I am a monkey
stuck in a tree
My mummy told me
it was too high for me.

I used to swing
from tree to tree
and drink from the
water hole,

I am a monkey
stuck in a tree
My mummy told
me it was too
high for me.

I would go out
and pick at
the nuts and
fruits and berries too.

I am a monkey
stuck in a tree
My mummy said
it was too high
for me.

I slipped and got
caught in a
branch
While running after
my brother.
I hate him really I
do.
Please set
me
free.

*Jennie Green  (10)*
*Millbrook Primary School*

# I AM A . . .

I am a dog
I am stuck in my kennel
I am howling all I can but nobody is coming.
They have shut me out all on my own,
I used to run and play all day long.

But now I am stuck in my kennel
I want to come out and eat my bone,
I want to go and play again,
I want to go for a long walk.

But now I am stuck in my kennel,
I used to like my family,
But now I am not sure,
Oh great! Here comes my owner,
With my lead and my ball.
(I like them really).

*Lucy Cripps  (9)*
*Millbrook Primary School*

# I Am A . . .

I am a dog
I'm stuck outside
It's dinnertime
So why am I outside?
I used to eat a potato or two.
I used to bring the Daily Mail.
I used to have a lovely meal
But I am stuck outside.
I used to get cuddles from
My master
But I am stuck outside.
I used to play in the living room
And sneak upstairs
And lick my master
And get in his bed.
But now I'm stuck outside.
I used to go for walks.
I'm beginning to feel that
I am in hell.

*Craig Gillott (9)*
*Millbrook Primary School*


# I Am A . . .

*Dolphin.*

I am a dolphin.
I am stuck in a net,
I used to swim and play,
I used to dance and sing.

I used to dive round coral reefs,
I used to tease fishes,
I used to hide from killer whales,
I used to jump round rowing boats.

But now I'm stuck in a net,
I can't swim and play,
I can't dance and sing,
I can't dive round coral reefs.

I can't tease fishes, they tease me,
I can't hide from killer whales,
I can't jump round rowing boats.

They're reeling me in,
I'm headed for the end.

*Jenny Yates (10)*
*Millbrook Primary School*


# I AM A COW

I am a cow,
I'm stuck in a shed
I am nearly always
In a very sad mood.
I used to walk in the
Fields all luscious and green.
But I am a cow,
Stuck in a shed.
I miss the sun,
Against my tum.
I miss the grass,
In a big mass.
I moo six sad moos
And I scream.
Grumble is my master
I hate him quite a lot
He knows I miss the field's green.
*Can't he understand?*

*Laura Yates (9)*
*Millbrook Primary School*

## I Am A Parrot

I'm a parrot
I live in a jungle
I never fall or never tumble,
I perch up high in a tree,
I live all day happy and free,
And at night I fly over the green forest canopy.

I'm a parrot,
I live in the jungle,
I never fall or never tumble,
I fly with the wind against my wing,
I like the nut
And the fruit picking.

I am a parrot,
I live in the jungle,
I never fall or never tumble,
I run, I walk,
I fly, I sing,
And I sparkle at night like a diamond ring.
I catch my bait,
And put it in a heap,
Then a midnight feast,
Then sleep . . . *zzzzzzz!*

*Jessica Dancy  (10)*
*Millbrook Primary School*

## I AM A MONKEY

I am a monkey,
I live in the trees,
I always enjoy the nice cool breeze.
I like to swing,
All light and free,
In the luscious
Green canopy.
I am a monkey,
I live in the trees,
I always enjoy the nice cool breeze.
I like the leaves that blow against my face,
And I like swinging at a very fast pace.
I am a monkey,
I live in the trees,
I always enjoy the nice cool breeze.
I screech, I talk,
I scream, I walk,
So if you come near me,
You better watch out,
Because I'll tease you if I can.
Tease you, tease you,
If I can.
I like it here, so,
I want to stay near.

*Lauren Marie Chessum  (9)*
*Millbrook Primary School*

## I AM A MOUSE

I am a mouse,
I am stuck in a cruel horrible mouse trap.
It squeezes my body as I struggle and fidget.
It just tightens,
I look high above me.
Giant monsters staring at me.
I remember when I roamed free,
I used to run and play,
I need to run free,
Time is ticking by.
Time seems to go quicker,
Only minutes,
Only seconds.
*Now I'm dead.*

**Rory McLean (9)**
**Millbrook Primary School**


## I AM AN EEL

I am an eel
I am stuck in a pond.
Carps are all over the place after eels.
Oh no, a carp has seen me.
I must swim, swim, swim for my life.
The carp is getting closer,
I am getting closer to the mill.
Now I'm up on the water wheel spinning
round and down, I fall into the water . . .
*Chomp! Crunch! Splatter!*

And that is the end of me.

**Stefan Overy (10)**
**Millbrook Primary School**

# I Am A . . .

I am a cheetah
I am stuck in a net
I used to run around
all day long
lying about in the hot day sun.

But now I'm stuck in a net
I used to run everywhere
I had such fun
playing with friends
enjoying the day
but now I can't even
move.

I'm very hot in the sun
starving with hunger
eating any insects
I see
for as the days go
past I get weaker
and weaker.

Before I was stuck
I used to find
loads of meat
and food
but now I'm
just going to
waste away.

*Kerry Revell (9)*
*Millbrook Primary School*

# I AM A . . .

I am a seal
I am stuck in a net.

I used to swim
I used to play
I used to dive for fish all day.

But I can't anymore
because I am stuck in a net.

I know what will be coming soon
the spear,
the dreaded spear.

It will come through the air
and cut the net
worse still, it will cut me
I will fall in the water
and die.

They want fish
they got me instead
here it comes
splash!
I'm dead.

*Claire Morris (9)*
*Millbrook Primary School*


# I AM A . . .

I am a hamster
I am stuck up a drainpipe
I am cold, hungry and wet all around.

I used to play in my ball
and I liked to tease the cat
I wish I could go back home.

Beneath me I can hear
my friends call me,
they sound so sad.
Well at least I have had a good life.
I can remember hiding under
all that sawdust.
But suddenly *bang! Whoosh!*
*Yippee!* I am out!

*Hollie Sawyer  (10)*
*Millbrook Primary School*


# I AM A . . .

I am a monkey
I am stuck in a tree
I miss all the wind
Brushing against me.

I am a monkey
I am stuck in a tree
Missing who I used to be
But now I am stuck in a tree.

I am a monkey
I am stuck in a tree
I used to play with all
My monkey friends but
Now I am stuck in a tree.

I am a monkey
I am stuck in a tree
Here comes the
Zoo keeper coming to
                get me.

*Shannon Lee Hetherington  (9)*
*Millbrook Primary School*

# I AM A . . .

I am a hamster.
I am stuck in a cage
I used to run in the field
Wash my paws and bathe in the sun

*but I am stuck in a cage!*

Up I climb
and my hard brown head
hits the top
so down I go
to the bottom at the beginning where
I started.

I used to run up and down
I used to go round and round the field
Above me the shadow of my owner
here he comes
to let me free.

**Chris Dunkley (9)**
**Millbrook Primary School**


# I AM A . . .

I am a spider
My leg is stuck under a stone
I struggle and squirm but it's too heavy for me
I wait for the
end of my lovely life.

I used to scare all the children away
and spin my wonderful web
but my leg is stuck under a stone
right at the end of a beach.

I see a child running
heading right for me
he comes and picks
the stone off me
and throws it in the sea.

For once I'm glad to see a child
then I crawl away
to my family
and tell them what happened
                              to me.

*Leila Kandola  (9)*
*Millbrook Primary School*


# I AM A . . .

I am a penguin
I'm stuck in the zoo
I used to swim freely
in the crystal sea.
I used to play with the sea lions
I rode on the backs of whales
I loved my old life
I am a penguin
I'm stuck in a zoo
All I do now is eat fish
I love to show off to loads of people
At night-time they take me out of the water
and put me in a tiny cage.
I really loved my old life
I miss my mum and dad
brother and sisters.
People throw things in the water
and I hate to swim in it.

*Amy Tompkins  (10)*
*Millbrook Primary School*

# I AM A . . .

I am a monkey
I am stuck in a tree
I used to eat all day
And swing in the trees.
I used to dodge from the hunters
But now I am stuck in a tree.
Up I jump out of the tree
But I hit a branch and fall back in.
I hear a branch crack on the floor
But it's just a snake.
I hear something else
What could it be? It's a hunter
*Bang! Bang! Bang!*
I fall to the floor, I am hit.
*I die.*

**Ben Danbury  (9)**
**Millbrook Primary School**


## YELLOW

Beautiful glistening sun
Cowslips growing in the meadows
With beautiful dandelions
Guiding my way.
Crisp sweetcorn
Tasting like butter
With beautiful warm sun
Peeping through the open window.

**Arran Attrill  (10)**
**Millbrook Primary School**

# I AM A . . .

I am a deer.
I am stuck in a tree with my antlers
I used to eat the lush green grass
And in the air the sweet smell of berries.

But I am stuck with my antlers.

I used to go out and play
With my friends in the thicket
I can see them playing
I wish I could go and play
But I am stuck with my antlers
All I usually eat is the lush long grass
But all I could eat now is the bark off this
Tree and that will not last long.

Oh no here comes a hunter
He cannot see me yet
Oh look there, someone is coming to help me.

The hunter has spotted me
He is taking aim
He cannot fire
The man has reached me.

*I'm free!*

I shall never forget him!

***Bethan Franklin  (9)***
***Millbrook Primary School***

## I AM A PARROT

I'm a parrot
I live free
out in the luscious canopy.
I fly around and around
all day looking for fruit to peck on.

I'm a parrot
I live free
out in the luscious canopy.
It's getting dark now I better fly back
I fly faster and faster until I get home
Oh no! I'm getting attacked.
Here I am lying here on the floor
ready to die.
Here comes my long lost owner
Let's hope he picks me up.
Back in my cage now,
all happy and safe.

*Jonathan Flint (9)*
*Millbrook Primary School*


## BLUE

Blue is like
the sea
rushing round
and round
the Earth.

*Splash! Splash! Splash!*
That's cold
it is rough
and wet.

Blue is like
ice
cold and shivery
makes your hand go
very very cold.

Blue is like jumpers
our school jumpers
Blue is really fun!

*Rebecca Hallwood (9)*
*Millbrook Primary School*

# I AM A . . .

I am a hamster
I am stuck in a hamster ball
I live in a cage
I live on my own
I'm always hungry
I don't like cats because they eat me
I crawl up to the ball lid but can't get out.
I am a hamster
I am stuck in a hamster ball
I see, oh I don't see, I do see . . . *Cat!*
The cat comes up and I try to get out
I can't, the lid is too strong.
I am a hamster
I am stuck in a hamster ball
I get the lid open, I run for dear life
The cat comes after me
I am saved, somebody left the cage open
I get in my cage and into my bed.

*Shelly Jade Pill (9)*
*Millbrook Primary School*

## I AM A KITTEN

I am a kitten
I am stuck in a tree.

I used to run and chase
but now I am nothing.

I have just missed lunch
Oh I love my lunch but I am stuck
and I cannot get down.
Look there are some birds.
I am so hungry I can eat anything.

I ache and I am so tired,
I feel like I'm going to fall.
I love my master, if only he
would come and save me.
It has been a week, I have only
eaten one bird.
I remember when I used to chase the children,
but I know I will never get down.
It has been nearly two weeks and nobody
                              has noticed me.
Oh look!
It's my master, he has come to save me!
*Miaow!*

*Nicol Haines  (10)*
*Millbrook Primary School*

116

# I AM A . . .

I am a puppy stuck in my kennel
I got told off for barking at the cat
I get no food.
There's a bone outside my kennel
my mouth is watering
I am a puppy stuck in my kennel all alone
there's my lead outside
And there's my owner coming towards me
He says 'Bad girl, no walk for you and no bone.'
One day later
My owner comes out of the house
he's got some food for me
and says 'You get your food but no walks.'
I am a puppy I have some food
but no walks.
Is it true my owner has come
with a bone?
*'Yum! Yum!'*
He says, but no walks.
I am a puppy, now my owner
takes me for walks
I have fun but every night
I go in my kennel.
now my owner lets me
stay out of my kennel
I rush into the house and see
everyone, and lie next
to the fire
and I got a very big bone.

*Leanne Wilkinson (9)*
*Millbrook Primary School*

## THE HEDGEHOG

It is only a little hedgehog
with about 100 spikes
If you touch it, it will pierce your skin
and make you bleed.
So only pick it up when you have got
gloves on.

But if you do pick it up
without gloves on you might catch
a disease
and it will hurt your hands.
So I'll only tell you once
So listen . . . 'Do not pick
a hedgehog up without gloves on
leave it alone.'

*Tony Tyler  (10)*
*Millbrook Primary School*


## I AM A . . .

I am a guinea-pig
trapped in my hutch.

I've never been out in my life.
I used to play with my friends
And have some fun,

But now I am trapped in my hutch

I am lonely all on my own
I miss my mum and dad
I specially liked the food

*But now I am trapped in my hutch!*

*Simon Cramp  (9)*
*Millbrook Primary School*

## I AM A . . .

I am a worm
I'm stuck on a hook
There's a hole in my stomach
All the blood trickles down
My stomach but it doesn't hurt.
Ow! Now he casts out
I wish I was still with my family
I used to play with worms
But now I'm stuck on a hook
All the water is going through my hole
                                  in my stomach.
Look! A fish!
*I am finished!*

***Tommy Hatton  (10)***
***Millbrook Primary School***


## MY PUP ALFIE

The softest brown eyes that just seem to say,
'I'll be good in a minute I just want to play.'

The silkiest ears that flap when he bounds,
Up and down fields and over the downs.

The waggiest tail that shows that he's happy,
He's always good-tempered, never snappy.

The largest paws, pink and chunky,
That dig up dad's garden, the little monkey!

All of these things just go to make up,
The naughtiest, wickedest, most adorable pup.

***Katie Baker  (11)***
***Our Lady's Convent Junior School***

## A VISIT FROM MARS

An alien came down from Mars and landed on our shed.
While sliding down the water pipe, he landed on his head.
He hopped up the path to our back door. He only had one leg.
He was a chatty sort of chap but I didn't catch a word he said.

I thought he might be hungry so I took him to the kitchen.
He didn't choose Mum's apple pie. I can't say that I blame him.
He jumped up on the table and then into the sink.
He found Mum's Fairy Liquid and thought he'd have a drink.

He turned a paler shade of green and I thought he might be sick.
I took him to the bathroom where he played a funny trick.
First he took the loo roll and wrapped it round his neck.
Then he found the toothpaste and guess what happened next?

He looked into our mirror and jumped out of his skin.
I picked it up from the bathroom floor and threw it in the bin.
This caused quite a commotion, Mum shouted 'What's to do?'
He gave me an enormous wink and I flushed him down the loo.

He popped out of the drainpipe and climbed back on the shed.
A spaceship came from Mars and took him home to bed.

*Anna Dziewulski  (11)*
*Our Lady's Convent Junior School*


## BABY BROTHER

I have a baby brother
His eyes are big and round,
He gets food from his mother
Just like any other.

He doesn't have a lot of hair
So please don't stare,
He's just like his father
Who doesn't have much to spare.

I love my baby brother
Although he doesn't talk,
He makes a lot of gurgles
And hasn't learnt to walk.

He loves it when I play with him
It keeps me fit and trim,
I don't need to go to the gym
Because he keeps me thin
He thinks everything is a game
But I love him all the same.

*Peter Hinton-Smith (10)*
*Our Lady's Convent Junior School*

## FLOWERS

Flowers of all colours,
Red, blue and green,
So good they just have to be seen.

Big, little, pretty-smelling,
Flowers of all shape and size,
Large, small, dainty and in disguise.

Flowers in the garden,
The first signs of spring,
Hidden bulbs, flowers they will bring.

Flowers for a wedding,
White for a bride,
Flowers being thrown at her side.

Flowers of all colours,
Purple, yellow and white,
Close up after dark and say 'Goodnight.'

*Imogen Maund (9)*
*Our Lady's Convent Junior School*

# The Nature Girl

Saddled on my horse, from my castle I go
My riding cape a fancy show
I'm searching for my dream come true
The grass is the greenest, the sky the best blue
In my hat a feather curl
The one I'm after is the Nature Girl

Others in the village small
Say she is not there at all
They say her dress is the pale blue sky
Her hair the rays of the sun high
But no, in my heart, deep down low
I hope I might think I know

She's there all the time needing a friend
Though all the animals she does tend
With loving hands she does care
But in her heart there is despair
For she's alone, no one around
Apart from the nature there is no sound

I ride along past valley and hill
My heart with joy and wonder fill
To see the nature running along
And hear the birds sing their love song
The animals meet and give a kiss
But the one I'm looking for is . . .

The girl dressed in satin blue
With golden hair down to the dew
On the grass which holds her slippered feet
And the moss cushions that are her seat
Her ear decorated with a delicate sea pearl
The one I'm after is the Nature Girl.

*Rebecca Harrison  (11)*
*Our Lady's Convent Junior School*

## MY PAINTBOX

White is the moon shining in the sky.
Bubbles floating in the bath,
Or an icy lake, cold and frosty,
My cold hands, shaking in the cruel icy wind.

Black might be outer space full of stars and planets
Or the dark night sky.
It might just be a drainpipe pushing water to the drain,
Or it could be a cave all dark and spooky.

Blue is the sky on a clear summer's day.
The sea bringing stones to the beach.
A big blue whale swimming in the deep blue sea,
Or a little fountain spouting out water.

Green is a long green snake slithering up a tree.
Grass in the summer.
Trees waving in the wind,
Or a crunchy apple all juicy and sweet.

Red is the sign of danger lurking round the corner,
The sun going down to bed,
The wine in my mother's glass,
Or butterflies that fly in the sky.

Yellow is the stars way up high
The cornfields exploding with corn.
Sunflowers that peep over the fence,
Or lemons all sour and sharp.

*Harriet Newman  (9)*
*Our Lady's Convent Junior School*

## POLLUTION (YEAR 2010)

Why, oh why, has the tiger gone?
I can now only see it in a book,
And the eagle, seal, wild cats and bears,
Have disappeared forever from sight.

Everywhere I look I see buildings,
Vehicles that pollute the air,
Noisy machines that pollute our world,
And trudging through litter on the way to school.

Our hobbies these days are playing on computers
And basically staying indoors,
Why bother going outside when there is
Nothing left to go out for?

In the history books we see lush, green grass,
Flowers and plants are growing,
Animals grazing,
What has man done to our earth to make it
                          like this?
Never will it be full of life again.

*Sophia Haynes  (9)*
*Our Lady's Convent Junior School*


## MY PONY BERTIE

I have a pony called Bertie,
Who is as sweet as sweet can be,
He stands in the corner all dirty,
I think he rolls especially for me.

I spend two hours grooming him,
Until his coat is gleaming,
Then we go for a canter,
And come back all steaming.

I give him a Polo after our ride,
His ears turn to prick,
I stare at my pony with love and pride,
And then he starts to lick.

*Lucy Larkman  (10)*
*Our Lady's Convent Junior School*


## COLOURS

Blue is sky on a summer's day
Rain wet but cool
Ocean smashing against the rocks
A deep wet pool.

Red is blood pouring down my arm
A juicy apple ready in the bowl
Flames dancing on the fire.

Black is sky at night
Coal ready to be burnt in a fire
A frightening storm
Or ashes from the fire.

Gold is the harvest moon
Ripe wheat swaying in the field
Treasure waiting to be found.

Yellow is the sun hot and bold
And the banana you eat every day.
Yellow is the colour of hair and hay.

Green is grass
And it might be leaves falling
Green is bushes swaying from side to side.

*Natalie Davis  (9)*
*Our Lady's Convent Junior School*

## WASHING MACHINE

I am a washing machine whizzing round and round
Making a horrible sound
Giving everyone a fright
Getting them out of my sight
Leaving me on my own
Time to be alone
Washing all their smelly socks
Giving me chickenpox
Thirty minutes later they come back to me
Saying *'Yippee!'*
All the clothes have been washed
And I look rather squashed
They now put a second set of clothes
For me to wash, *oh no!*

*Denise Kemp  (10)*
*Our Lady's Convent Junior School*


## WILD PONIES

Wild ponies galloping round,
Over hills they leap and bound.

They're never tamed, have a will of steel,
Rolling round, just like wheels.

A stallion, mare, foal and colt,
Kicking, neighing, 'bout to bolt.

*Elspeth Gillespie  (10)*
*Our Lady's Convent Junior School*

# My Computer

My computer has a mouse, but it does not eat cheese,
It plays games with me, but is not my friend,
It has ram, but it does not have sheep,
It has chips, but it is never hungry.

It has a keyboard, but it does not play music,
It is clever, but not intelligent,
It has a footprint, but has no feet,
It has memory but cannot think.

It has heads, but no hair,
It plays discs, but does not listen to music
It has speakers, but does not talk,
It has a joystick, but it does not fly.

***Philip Thomas (9)***
***Our Lady's Convent Junior School***


# The Grandfather Clock

The old, dusty shadow-like figure
Stands lonely in the corner,
While the muffled pendulum swings smoothly
Making the stiff hands move
The numbers stay there covered with dirt
While cobwebs surround its face,
But the clock will never stop
Like time will never end.

***Megan Madden (10)***
***Our Lady's Convent Junior School***

## SPACE

One day my mother said
'We are going on a journey to space
in a rocket flying high,
to see the planets in the sky.'
The next day I got in a rocket,
with a green point at the top.
When I was up, up in the sky,
I waved to another spaceship passing by.
We went to Mars to have our lunch
and, then to the moon for tea.
Then I woke up, it was all a dream
and there was no rocket with a
green point at the top,
only my bed all warm and cosy,
with my blanket on the top.

*Laura Dziewulski (8)*
*Our Lady's Convent Junior School*


## POLLUTION AND LITTER

Pollution and litter are the things we all hate,
People leave litter under the gate.

Car pollution breaks the ozone layer,
People leave litter just anywhere.

Car pollution we could do without,
Litter we could avoid no doubt.

Tins that we throw away,
We could recycle to use another day.

*Lucy Whitehead (10)*
*Our Lady's Convent Junior School*

## WINTER DAY

W oolly coat and woolly hat,
I   cy cold toes,
N ice warm cosy inside,
T  hat's the way it goes,
E  veryone's freezing cold,
R  oaring fire keeps me warm.

D  ays go by, winter's old,
A  nd then one early morn,
Y  ippee! Spring has come!

*Helena Todd  (10)*
*Our Lady's Convent Junior School*

## THE CAT

Searching for food raiding bins,
She sneaks and passes moonlit inns.
She smells a mouse running by,
Slowly she creeps like a spy.
Ready to pounce, she's standing still
She does a cry, high and shrill.
Oh no, there's a dog on its way
So the cat quickly runs away.

*Andrée Latham  (9)*
*Our Lady's Convent Junior School*

## IF I RULED THE WORLD

If I ruled the world I would make sure
that no one would fight and no one was poor.

If I ruled the world I would make sure
that no one would kill animals for their tusks and their skin,
and in my world they would live happily within.

If I ruled the world I would make sure
that wildlife was happy and always secure
and that people lived safely without the worry of war.

If I ruled the world I would make sure
that no one had to live on the street
and everyone had enough to eat.

If I ruled the world I would make sure
that all children had a mum and dad,
and that all of them were lucky enough to have
had all the love that I have had.

*Erin Murphy  (9)*
*Peppard CE Primary School*


## GOLD

A beautiful ring.
Shining pound coins.
My mummy's buttons on her coat.
A sparkling crayon.
Hard metal cymbals.
Lovely ribbons.
The beads on my silk hair band.
The runny ink in a pen.

*Amy Wilkins  (8)*
*Peppard CE Primary School*

## QUESTIONS

What is the moon?
A shining great biscuit.
Why do cats have tails?
They'd look silly without one.
What's inside a mountain?
Cavemen hacking at rocks.
What are waves?
Presents for surfboarders.
What are clouds?
Candy floss that doesn't want to be eaten.
What do policemen do when they are alone?
He puts speeding tickets on all the cars.
Why is the grass green?
It is the cow's favourite colour.
What is the sun?
One of Hitler's gas bombs that got stuck up in the sky.

*Is life a dream?*
*To me it is.*

*Edward Rule  (7)*
*Peppard CE Primary School*

## THE GREAT DRAGON

The dragon leaps up in the air.
Its yellow and pink hair flows in the wind.
I like to see it dancing and leaping all around.
Its sparkling patterns flow on its scales.
The spikes are all spotty.
Its claws are sharp.
The jaws open and close and fire comes out
of them.

*Hannah Stevenson  (8)*
*St Andrew's School*

## BONFIRE NIGHT

Rockets whooshing up in the air,
Making the sound of a hungry bear.

Volcanoes so light and bright,
Lighting up the dark, dull night.

Golden rain, what a pretty sight!
Always looking so very bright.

What about the Catherine wheel?
That looks like it's rolling down a hill.

What about the bonfire bright?
Looking bright in the dark, dark night.

*Jonathan Cooper (9)*
*St Andrew's School*


## DRAGONS

See all the dragons
Dance through the town.
See the swirly, curly,
Spotty patterns on its back.
The fearsome dragon
Pounced at the people.
The angry dragon breathed
Fire out of his nose.
The dragon pounced again,
The dragon goes around the
Street to look for children -
To make friends.

*Charlotte Ward (7)*
*St Andrew's School*

## WHERE I LIVE

I live in a house
That sits in a village
And the village
Sits in a county.
The county sits in a country and
The country sits in a continent.
The continent sits in
The earth and
The earth sits in
A solar system.
The solar system sits in
The galaxy and
The galaxy sits in
The universe.
But I sit in a little place in
All of this
And I am glad I do.

*William Blackshaw (19)*
*St Andrew's School*


## DRAGONS

See all the dragons,
Spiky and fierce.
Pouncing on everyone.
It blows smoke and fire.
It swirls around and around.
It goes down the street,
And scares everyone away.
Its jaws are sharp.
It gobbles little girls up!

*Melissa Allen (7)*
*St Andrew's School*

# FIREWORKS

Fireworks are noisy,
Noisy and bright,
Fireworks are colourful,
Colourful and bright.

Some fireworks whiz,
Whiz through the air.
Fireworks are fun,
Fun at night.

Rockets go up,
Up in the air.
When they stop -
They bang!

Catherine wheels go round,
Round and round.
Fireworks are fun,
Fun at night.

*Annabel Clark  (9)*
*St Andrew's School*

# MY FAVOURITE DRAGON

My dragon leaps up into the air.
I see him dancing everywhere.
His colours are red and blue,
Grey, pink, orange, green, purple, brown,
His jaws are big and sharp and pointy,
His sparkly patterns flow in the air,
His curly skin is soft and smooth.
I like my dragon a lot.

*Eloise Jenkins  (8)*
*St Andrew's School*

## DRAGONS

See all the dragons,
Dancing down the street.
Look at that one.
It has flashing eyes.
And blazing fire.
It's got spotty wings.
And ferocious jaws.
It has a spiky tail.
It's swirling everywhere.
See all the dragons.
Dancing down the street.

*Clare Gent  (7)*
*St Andrew's School*

## STRESS

I feel stress,
It goes between your toes
It goes right to your nose,
     Stress,
I hate stress,
It's like a really long dress,
     Sleep,
I love sleep, a really long sleep,
Now that's a promise I will keep
     Sleep.

*Emma Clarke  (9)*
*St Andrew's School*

# POLLUTION

Pollution is so bad,
It makes me feel so sad.

It's clogging up the air,
Here, there, everywhere.

The air used to be blue,
All lovely and new.

But now it's grey,
Ever greyer than yesterday!

But it is slowly destroying us,
Bit by bit, dust by dust.

But if you want to stop it,
We're going to have to hop it.

It's numbering our days,
In lots of different ways.

And it's our own mess,
And it's not the best.

There are so many fumes,
It's going in the tubes.

It really needs to go,
Are we friend or foe?

Do we really need to inhale?
It makes us go so pale.

The air used to be so clean,
The atmosphere so green.

When have I ever seen,
The air so fresh and clean?

But hey!
We can make a difference some day.

*Anna-Louise Gibson  (11)*
*St Andrew's School*

## PEACE

Saddam Hussein is insane.
He is the one to blame,
He thinks it's all one big game.

We would like peace,
But the problems seem to increase.

We have enough natural disaster,
Without any more,
The world is not for war.

Children will cry
If their fathers go to war,
And mothers will sigh
When their beloveds go to war.

We have already
Had two world wars,
We do not need any more!

*Gloria Tempest-Mogg  (11)*
*St Andrew's School*

# FUMES

Fumes, fumes, fumes.
I hate fumes!
I wish I could
Do something about it.
So many cars,
So many fumes,
I can hardly breathe.
I wish I could think
Of a car that would
Not pollute the earth.
Scientists have thought
Of an electric car,
But it hasn't worked yet!
I know cars are useful
But please think about this,
Why don't you cycle,
Or take a brisk walk.
If you don't, just be careful,
Just think about all the animals,
Just think about all the birds,
Soon we'll have no animals,
Soon we'll have no birds.
So hurry up scientists
Think of something quick!

*Victoria Bracey (11)*
*St Andrew's School*

## FRIENDS

Friends, friends, all sorts of friends.
Some fat,
Some thin,
Some tall,
Some lean,
But they're all the same,
Unless they're mean!

Some friends are sad,
Some happy,
Some mad!
But the thing is,
At least we have friends!

Sisters, brothers,
And all the ot hers,
Where would we be without them?
I'll tell you -
We would be at war,
One and all,
If it weren't for friends.

*Jessica Dunsdon  (10)*
*St Andrew's School*

## WHEN'S BONFIRE NIGHT? (NOT YET!)

Mummy, when's bonfire night?
Not yet son, it's only October.

Mummy now is it bonfire night?
Look son, nearly!

Daddy, when's bonfire night?
Well, it's the 1st November today
So that means, nearly.

Daddy now is it bonfire night?
Leave me, I'm working.
Ask Mum.

Mum have you seen my sister, Sally?
She's upstairs.

Sally, when's bonfire night?
Tomorrow is bonfire night.

Mum have you seen my brother Tim?
He's outside.

Tim, when's bonfire night?
I'm dying to know.
It's tonight, silly.
Yes!

Come on Mum, it's bonfire night,
Let's have a good time.

*Natalie Vincent (10)*
*St Andrew's School*

# MY FRIEND CAMILLA

My friend Camilla,
I call her Milly.
Her hair is long and brown,
A bit like mine.
She has blue-grey eyes,
Just like mine.
She lives in Lambourn,
Quite near me.

She is fun to have around,
Milly said I am too.
She can be a bit naughty,
But not as naughty as me!
She is quite kind,
I hope I am too.
She is not lazy,
Just like me.

She has a border terrier, Winkle,
We have its sister, Pebbles.
Winkle always jumps the last three stairs,
But ours doesn't.
She has her own horse,
It must be hard to look after.
My friend Milly
Is a good friend for me.

*Hayley Dyer (10)*
*St Andrew's School*

## WHERE I LIVE

I live in a house
That's to the west of you,
It's a beautiful house you'll like,
And I do, too.

The house is in a village
And the village is fairly small,
The geese from the pond walk up the street,
Not minding the cars at all.

My house has a name called Cedarwood,
It has a garden as well,
Behind the garden is a big, big field.
Which the farmer would like to sell.

My favourite place is the attic,
It's creepy and scary up there.
Or it could be the bathroom,
Where I always comb my hair!

I s'pose wherever we live is home,
Despite where we wander or roam.
I hope you have got my message,
There's nothing quite like *Home Sweet Home!*

**Richard Soames  (10)**
**St Andrew's School**

# PEACE

Peace, peace is a lovely thing
The sound of it has a comforting ring,
Unless we take a lot more trouble . . .
All that we have, will burst like a bubble.

Peace, peace is a lovely thing
Around the world it's spread like a wing,
We are so lucky we have so much
It's one of those things we cannot touch.

War, war is a terrible thing
It causes lots of suffering,
Lives are wrecked and homes are lost
It all comes down to an awful cost.

War, war is a terrible thing
Hitler was the war king,
Saddam Hussein could be the same
If we let him play his game.

Peace, peace is what we need
An end to fighting, dying and greed,
If there isn't, we won't have peace
And pointless war will never cease.

Peace, peace is what we need
To keep it we must do our deed,
If we are all kind at heart
The spreading of peace will make a start.

*Alex Powis (9)*
*St Andrew's School*

## WHERE I LIVE

We live in Seven Barrows
And in the garden we grow marrows.
My daddy has some horses which
Run at all the racecourses.

We have a lot of grass,
Which makes the horses go fast.
And the tractors work all day,
Moving straw and making hay.

In the wild we have moles and bats,
And hedgehogs and some rats.
But I prefer my cats because
They catch the rats.

But over there is a goat in the stable,
And the horse called Mabel.
In the summer we go in the pool
And this keeps me nice and cool.

*Camilla Henderson (10)*
*St Andrew's School*


## PAINTING

A sleek lick of paint runs across the smooth
surface of a piece of paper.
Portraits and landscapes.
Impressionists and expressionists.
Oil paints and water paints.
Dots and lines dash across the paper.
Faces spring out of the shimmering colours.
Flowers jump out of the shaded greens.

*Balan Evans (10)*
*St Mary's CE Primary School*

## THE WRITER OF THIS POEM

The writer of this poem
Is as tall as a tree,
As wise as the wisest owl,
Just like you and me.

She's as keen as a hitch hiker
Is as clever as brainy Billy,
As friendly as a cuddly bear,
And definitely silly.

The writer of this poem
Is as pretty as can be,
As quick as a shooting rocket,
That you can hardly see.

*Ashlee Rose  (10)*
*St Mary's CE Primary School*

## COSMIC COSMO

Cosmic Cosmo
Out there in space
Seeing sights on Mars
Icarus and Sicarus.

His spaceship flies at a magnificent pace,
Making the land speed record, only a trace.

Monthly Mars bars
Giant Milky Ways
He never gets hungry
Or so my dad says.

*Daniel Howard  (10)*
*St Mary's CE Primary School*

## I WISH

I wish I could fly away
onto an island so far away.
So no one could bother me.

I wish I could be in a 'rock band'
playing on the drums.
And be a helping hand.

I wish I could be the 'Men In Black'
going around,
bustin' aliens.

I wish I could ride Apollo 30
and go the moon,
and leave footprints.

I wish, I wish that this would
come true.
Oh come true.

*Thomas Jordan  (9)*
*St Mary's CE Primary School*


## CHRISTMAS

Christmas tree,
Happy Christmas everyone.
Ripping open the presents.
I enjoy Christmas dinner.
Snapping Christmas crackers.
Tearing the presents.
Merry Christmas, Mum
And people like Christmas
Sniffing the lovely dinner.

*Katie Harris  (10)*
*St Mary's CE Primary School*

## I'D LIKE TO . . .

I'd like to
fly in a 'hornet' and
zoom on the enemy.
Be like the wind
have a race with sound
and with light.
But everybody knows I will win.

I'd like to
march with the army
train with them too.
Shoot with the army
but everybody knows I'll fail.

*Gregory Wooldridge  (10)*
*St Mary's CE Primary School*


## I WALK INTO A GARDEN

I walk into a magnificent garden
Full of bright and colourful flowers
All shapes and sizes
Beautiful scents whoosh up my nose
On my left, there's a weeping willow
On my right there's a little stream
In the weeping willow there's a small swing
I sit on the swing
And swing myself gently in the country air
I decide to take a little paddle
In the gently rippling stream.

*Molly Pryke  (10)*
*St Mary's CE Primary School*

## THE BLACK BEAST

As the dark, black clouds come over the hill.
Looks like ghosts are coming to kill.
Then they fade away.
Because the black beast comes out to prey.
The birds go in.
And so does day.
The beast doesn't like light or day.
So when the moon and stars come out.
The beast is never about.

*Kirsty Robson  (10)*
*St Mary's CE Primary School*


## THE HAUNTED HOUSE

A great looming tree has a great looming hand,
The house has dust like golden sand.
I looked over my shoulder, I saw something there,
It was big, green and ugly, but it had no hair.
I ran faster and faster, but he gained on me,
Then all of a sudden, I bumped into that tree!

*Scott Warner  (9)*
*St Mary's CE Primary School*


## SLOWLY

Slowly the snail slithers across the ground
Slowly it slithers without a sound.
Slowly it moves, leaving a trail.
He's got a hard shell which saves him from hail.
Slowly, slowly a baby is born.
Slowly grows the rhino's horn.

*Christopher Mason  (10)*
*St Mary's CE Primary School*

## PRIVATE DETECTIVE

Sneakily the private detective
Suspiciously sneaks around.
Sneakily the private detective
Is amazingly dangerously
on a case.
Sneakily he looks around
hoping to find another clue.
Then he hears a cry of laughter.
Then he gets the man he is looking for.
So that means the case is solved.

*Daniel Hanks  (9)*
*St Mary's CE Primary School*


## THE BIG MOVE

There is a team called Sunderland
who played at Roker Park
The ground was surrounded by houses
and was always dim and dark.

A new stadium was needed
It had to be big and bright
The fans' votes were needed
It was named the Stadium Of Light

At this time of the year,
near the top of Division One,
they can see the light.
The Premier League is the reason,
that things are looking bright,
for next season - in the Stadium Of Light.

*Colm Cummings  (10)*
*St Mary's RC Primary School*

## FOOTBALL CRAZY

I'm football crazy, I'm football mad
If it's to do with football, I'll go mad
Football is my life, it brings me no strife

Football is the game, that's full of fame

Arsenal are the best, better than all the rest
Completely untouchable, that's why they beat 'em all
I have all the Arsenal stuff, they're the team that never bluff

Football is the game, that's full of fame

I have footy posters and video games
Books, videos and even board games
I collect stickers and cards too

I play for a club, they're definitely not bad
And as you can see I'm . . .

*Footy mad!*

**Kevin Markwell  (11)**
**St Mary's RC Primary School**


## SPORT

*S* wimming is tough.
*P* ing-pong is fun,
*O* lympics are hard,
*R* ugby is rough,
*T* ennis is tiring as well as the rest.
　　But I like sport and sport is the *best!*

**Sean Northfield  (10)**
**St Mary's RC Primary School**

# MY FIRST DAY AT SCHOOL

I remember when I was four, when my mama
took me to my new school;
I was too shy for a start, but so excited within
my heart.

I couldn't wait to go to school, and tell my
friends about the rule;
You'll never guess how much I felt, I was just
hoping for the best.

And so I went on my first day, and met some
children on the way,
They maybe thinking what I think, that a school
is just for learning and fun.

So in the class where I belong, kids are smiling,
they look too exciting,
The teacher was kind of strict, but fair to all
the pupils' needs.

The lessons were so tricky and fun and really it
was just a charm,
How I enjoyed on my first day and we're still
learning all the way.

Never have I, missed school, unless of course
when I'm ill and poorly;
That is one thing I am proud of, 'cause someday
I know I'll have something to show off.

Believe me when I say these things, you won't
go wrong even a bit;
Forever you will benefit, the career you've chosen
would make you rich.

*Andrea Hart  (10)*
*St Mary's RC Primary School*

## SWIMMING

It's my favourite sport
It's wet,
It's fast,
But you can't take your pet.

There's front,
There's back,
There's butterfly,
And breast-stroke.

You can dive,
You can jump,
It's fun,
So long as you don't get the hump.

But what is this sport I talk of?
What is this,
Fun,
Fast, wet sport?

Take a guess,
It's fun, it's wet
You can dive.
*It's swimming!*

*Felicity Martin  (10)*
*St Mary's RC Primary School*

## The Clever Guys

The clever guys, the clever guys,
They know a thing or two.
But when they start thinking,
Their thoughts go down the loo!

For years and years the clever guys knew,
The thought was very dim.
To sail the seven seas because,
You might fall off the rim!

Those guys again they built a ship,
They knew it couldn't sink.
Its name was the *Titanic,*
What happened? What do you think!

All the time the clever guys knew,
They would have bet a pound.
That the sun went round the Earth,
And, not the other way round!

So there you are, so there it is,
Those guys are not so bright.
Is this a clever poem?
Have *I* got it right?

*Kieran Gallagher (11)*
*St Mary's RC Primary School*

# CATS

Cats are careful
Cats are clean
Cats are playful
Cats like cream.

Cats are tidy
Cats are messy
Cats are greedy
Cats are needy.

Cats are loving
Cats are mean
Cats are nothing
Cats are everything.

Cats are happy
Cats are sad
Cats are batty
Cats are mad.

I love cats,
I think they love me
All sorts of cats
Especially mine!

*Harriet Harwood  (11)*
*St Mary's RC Primary School*

# DEMI AND ME . . .

Up I go higher and higher . . .
The fluffy white clouds all around me.
Squadron Leader Murphy, fighter pilot - that's me!

Her engine roars like fighting lions -
Her wings soar like an eagle's span.
Demi, my plane, is like a shiny new can.

Out we go to test her -
With all the other planes.
Far, we go, away from sea, sand or land.

The air gets colder the higher we go,
And thinner than a piece from a silky bow.
Demi gives me the oxygen mask and,
I know I'll be safe.

The test flight is over, down we must go!
I handle her smoothly, as we hit the
Rough, bumpy land.
Off comes my mask when the lions die.
And I polish her shine with my leather gloved hand.

By: 514629 Squadron Leader C N Murphy (3 Squadron RAF)

*Claire Murphy  (11)*
*St Mary's RC Primary School*

## SEASONS OF THE HORSE

Thundering hooves smashing ice,
Falling off isn't that nice,
Riding fast wind in hair,
Jumping high in the winter air,
Stables are cosy,
Even while the horses are nosy.

Sweaty hack,
Sticky tack,
Heavy tails swatting flies,
Underneath the clear blue skies,
Stomping hooves on the sun-baked earth,
The horse is sweating around his girth.

Mud squelching, rain in eyes,
Trotting along under clouded skies,
Safe in the stable out of the rain,
Combing the raindrops out of his mane,
Splashing through puddles my horse and me,
Nearly time to go home and have tea.

*Anna Mee  (9)*
*St Mary's RC Primary School*


## MY PET DOG MINNIE

My pet dog Minnie
Used to be so skinny
But now she's old and grey;
The thin bits have gone away.

She's white and black
Has had a heart attack
Plenty of life is in her though,
Because the vet has told me so.

When she was young she would run for miles
Jump over fences, gates and stiles;
Chase birds, rabbits and silly cats,
She's even been known to chase some bats.

She has a big bed
Where she rests her head.
She is my friend,
Until the very end.

*Felicity A Nichols  (9)*
*St Mary's RC Primary School*


## ICE HOCKEY

Ice hockey is really good
You will enjoy it like a pud.

We will always laugh and cheer
Sometimes men will have a beer.

When the away-team lose
Sometimes we will hear some boos.

The puck might come flying in the air
It can hurt you like a bear.

The players' skates are pretty nifty
They will cost more than £150.

Their sticks are really tall and big
They are much thinner than a pig.

When we win, people might really sing
If we lose, people might get in a mood.

When we go and see a game
Win or lose, we love it just the same.

*Stephanie Trott  (10)*
*St Mary's RC Primary School*

## PRESENTS

I like presents, I don't try to be greedy
but I can't help it, I feel like I am needy.
So on my birthday every year,
I try my best, it's quite clear,
to be good and have no fear,
for I shall get something dear.
The paper and bow I tear.
The box is opened -
What is it in there?
A toy or something to wear?
A game or new teddy bear?
That's why I'm happy to get presents,
getting gifts is always pleasant.
So when I'm good
I think it's understood
that goodness is its own reward.
But getting presents
is even better.

*Holly Beyerle  (9)*
*St Mary's RC Primary School*


## SWIMMING

*S*   wimming is fun,
*W*   ith lifeguards you are safe,
*I*   n blue water you can swim in lanes,
*M*   eet your friends,
*M*   ake a splash.
*I*   n the showers the water is warm,
*N*   ear the edge there are tiles,
*G*   et fit, I love swimming!

*Carol McLeish  (10)*
*St Mary's RC Primary School*

# INKY

I have a cat called Inky
He is a jolly chap.
This year he will be 17
I'm not as old as that!

He wears a furry coat
It's mostly black and white.
His tail goes sort of spiky
When he gets a fright.

Although his coat is black
He has four white feet.
It looks as if he wears socks
And it looks quite neat.

He has green eyes
They look a bit like mine.
He's always climbing the trees
But still goes to bed at nine.

In the summertime
He tries to catch a mouse.
If he is successful
He brings it back to the house!

He eats a lot of food
He has a litter tray.
Dad is in charge of that
Not me, *no way!*

***Thomas Tennant (11)***
***St Mary's RC Primary School***

## TEDDY BEARS

*Teddies* are big, *teddies* are small
I don't care because I love them all.

*Teddies* can be really soft, I have two
              with me at night
Digger is very old, but he stops me getting
                  a fright.

I've got lots of *teddies* in my bedroom,
If I had them all in my bed
There wouldn't be any room for me, not even
                my head.

I have big *teddies*, small *teddies,* huge -
*Teddies*, tiny *teddies* and even *teddies* to
            fit in my pockets.

*Christine Pring  (10)*
*St Mary's RC Primary School*


## A YOUNG GIRL'S DANCE DREAM

Skimming about in the kitchen
Wishing, if only, I could go.

Dancing about in the kitchen,
Trying to remember, 'good toes, naughty toes'.

Worrying about exams in the kitchen
Lower-grade one, today.

Feeling pleased in the kitchen,
Passing the exam,
Shame, 'twas only a
           Dream!

*Ellen Carey  (10)*
*St Mary's RC Primary School*

## SWIMMING

I like swimming
in the sea.
I like swimming
in the pool.
I like swimming
because it's fun.
I like swimming
because we can dive.
I like swimming
because it makes my hair go frizzy.
I like swimming
because we can splash.
I like swimming
because we can learn.
I like swimming
because we can jump.
I like swimming
because we can swim.
I like swimming
because it's really good.

*Frances McIntyre (9)*
*St Mary's RC Primary School*


## DOCTORS

D oing what they can
O perating to save lives
C aring for people
T reating the wound
O xygen to help you breathe
R emoving bullets and things.

*Antony Coggins (10)*
*St Mary's RC Primary School*

## SANTA

Santa comes down the chimney in red,
While both me and Claire are sleeping in bed.
He sometimes puts presents under the tree,
For all my family including me.
On his sleigh he has no gears,
But one thing he has, is four reindeers.
We put three or four carrots out for the reindeers,
But now look what Santa's found, four or five beers.
He goes around to the children at night,
But only gives presents if they don't fight.
Santa is clever, magic too,
He gives presents to each one of you.

*Amy Knight-Archer  (10)*
*St Mary's RC Primary School*


## SPIDERS

*S*  piders scampering up the walls.
*P*  laying and weaving in their webs.
*I*  nteresting creatures so misunderstood.
*D*  ancing legs across the floor.
*E*  xciting patterns in their webs.
*R*  ound and black, with creepy legs.
*S*  pinning webs so eagerly for us to see.

*Amy Truby  (11)*
*St Mary's RC Primary School*


## SWIMMING

Swimming, swimming in a swimming pool;
Front stroke, back stroke, any stroke is cool.
When it comes to diving, I think that it's best;
Sometimes I just feel like, swimming in my vest.

I'd go swimming anywhere;
Even in the heather.
Nothing could ever stop me,
Apart from treacherous weather.

*Shaun James Moss  (10)*
*St Mary's RC Primary School*


## THE BOX

The box
Is as cunning as the cunning fox.
In daytime it is a sleeper - until,
It wakes at the remote control's will.
Then its face is ablaze
Showing us the latest craze.
People talking,
Models walking
Down the catwalk.
And yet there's more talk.
Football players run
Cricketers in the sun.
The contenders fight
Against the gladiators' might.
Flashing here
And flashing there
The box is going everywhere.
Anywhere you want to be,
The box will take you - just you see!
At night the box will go away
Until it wakes, another day.

*David Head  (9)*
*St Mary's RC Primary School*

## FOOTBALL

Football is rubbish,
It really is a bore.
Rugby is the best,
When we play, we get full score.

Footballers fall all over the floor,
Like big babies, for nothing at all.
But rugby players do touch the floor,
'Cos rugby's tough, unlike football.

Yes I said that they are babies,
The ball they have is round,
It is like a baby's rattle,
But it doesn't make a sound.

*James Kelly  (10)*
*St Mary's RC Primary School*


## SWEETS

Sweets can be any shape
Sometimes round and juicy
Sweets can be different flavours
Peppermint or maybe fruity.

My favourite ones are toffee
Even though they're not good for me.
I have them with my coffee
And sometimes with my tea.

The dentist said I shouldn't
That really is a shame,
But Santa said I could
So I eat them just the same.

*Caroline Winter  (9)*
*St Mary's RC Primary School*

## MY TEDDY BEAR

My teddy bear,
I take him everywhere
He has only got one ear,
So he can't really hear.
We do everything together
In any kind of weather,
My teddy and me.

I take him to bed every night
Say my prayers and hold him tight.
I've had him since I was three
I love him and he loves me.

My teddy
and me.

*Fay Coogan (9)*
*St Mary's RC Primary School*


## MUM

Mum, she is the number one
and at the end of the day
I love her in every way.

Unfortunately I'm not always good
and if I don't go the right way
she will make me pay.

Many times I have been bad
but she forgave me
and I am very glad.

*Daniel Smith (10)*
*St Mary's RC Primary School*

## MY TEACHER

You are jolly kind and good,
Always in a happy mood.
Teacher this is specially for you
Thanks for helping me at school.

Teacher, Teacher don't be mad
Sorry if we make you sad
Keep smiling keep laughing,
You are the best,
If it wasn't for you we'd fail our tests.

When home time comes,
We are all so sad.
But you must be glad 'ha, ha' to see us go
I don't think that is really so!

*Leanne Guess  (9)*
*St Mary's RC Primary School*

## THE SASQUATCH

There are some creatures called the sasquatch.
In a bush or in a tree, they like to watch us curiously.
They are sometimes spotted by a creek.
They can also be found on a mountain peak.
They are big and hairy - like people
That are nearly as tall as a church steeple.
They appear to be kind, but somehow look scary.
I'm sure this reaction makes them feel wary.
Perhaps someday they'll want to be discovered.
This would make me quite happy.
Until then, the sasquatch's life will have to remain covered.

*Cory Doerr  (9)*
*St Mary's RC Primary School*

## MY PET RABBIT

My pet rabbit Patch
is very hard to catch.
He hops like mad
and annoys my dad.
He eats lots of food
when he's in a hungry mood,
He is very hyperactive
and also very attractive.
He's never sad
he's always glad.
He hears with his long tall ears
then I say 'I love you very much.
It's time to put you back in your hutch.'

*Maria McGrogan  (9)*
*St Mary's RC Primary School*


## SUMMER

Summer's coming here again,
Leaves are sprouting on the trees,
Flowers growing everywhere,
Big and bright and colourful,
Birds are singing tweet, tweet, tweet,
Bees and buzzing buzz, buzz, buzz,
The sun is shining warm and brightly,
Everybody's at the beach,
In and out the sea they go,
The waves are whooshing high and low.
Everybody's having fun,
In the nice warm sun.

*Katie Lockyer  (9)*
*St Mary's RC Primary School*

## MY TEDDY BEAR

Cutie Pie is my best friend.
She never lets me down.
I tell her all my tales of woe,
and she comforts me when I am low.
When we go out, we wear matching bows
and we both love, changing our clothes.
She is furry and cuddly,
and has beautiful blue eyes.
I love her dearly.
She is clever and wise.

*Elizabeth Cummings  (9)*
*St Mary's RC Primary School*


## SIX LITTLE MONKEYS

Six little monkeys on a summer's day
one packed its bags and ran away.
Five little monkeys swing in a tree
one fell down and broke his knee.
Four little monkeys eating bananas
one fell and landed on the farmers.
Three little monkeys wearing glasses
one fell over as owner passes.
Two little monkeys both aged seven
one died and went to heaven.
One little monkey all alone,
sat in the garden and turned to stone.
No little monkeys playing around
end of story never be found.

*Anita Preston  (9)*
*Uffington Primary School*

## THE PAPERCLIP MONSTER

There's a paperclip!
That's only one
Where are the others?
Where are the others?
Boxes and boxes come in the class each day,
But they're not there the next day.
Where have they gone?
Maybe a monster comes out in the night to eat them.
Maybe the children just fiddle about with them.
It remains a mystery,
And it probably always will.
But I still like to think a monster eats them.

*Michael Usher  (10)*
*Uffington Primary School*

## CHRISTMAS TONGUE TWISTER

Santa's sleigh slides on slick snow.
Bryan brings big bright bells.
Santa stuffs Stephie's striped stocking.
Running reindeer romp around red wreaths.
Tiny Tommy climbs the tall tree with tinsel.
Chipper chilly children cheerfully chant.
Sunday Santa sang silly songs.
Eleven elves lick eleven little liquorice lollipops.
Comet cuddles cute Christmas kittens carefully.
Two trains travel together to Toyland.
Santa's sack sags slightly.
Ten tiny trains toot ten times.

*Natalie Russ  (10)*
*Uffington Primary School*

## 10 FOOTBALL PLAYERS

Ten football players standing in a line
one fell over then there were nine.
Nine football players jumped over a gate
one caught his knee then there were eight.
Eight football players wanted to play in heaven
one got his wish then there were seven.
Seven football players made some concrete mix
two fell in, then there were five.
Five football players smashed through a door
one was hurt then there were four.
Four football players went to swat a bee
one got stung, then there were three.
Three football players said to a cow 'Moo'
it was a bull, then there were two.
Two football players went for a marathon run,
one ran too far, then there was one.
One football player all alone,
no football match today so he went home.

*Thomas Lloyd  (9)*
*Uffington Primary School*


## WHERE HAVE ALL THE PAPERCLIPS GONE?

Where have all the paperclips gone?
Don't ask me, I'm asking you.
Don't tell me you took them with you
When you went to the loo!

Where have all the paperclips gone?
You haven't dropped them on the floor,
Or hoovered them up as well.
You'd better have found them all
Before I count to four!

Where have all the paperclips gone?
Who's got them, have you?
I did find some in the toilet,
Don't tell me you did take them with you!

Where have all the paperclips gone?
Please tell me, please tell me do,
I have found out the truth,
You did take them, didn't you?

*Jennifer Long  (9)*
*Uffington Primary School*


## SKATING COMPETITION

On my way to a skating competition.
I was nervous when I arrived.
I had a practise on the ice,
I felt sleepy,
it was only 5.20am.
Getting ready to skate
clean, white boots
with a white net skirt.
Hair and make-up all done
I was ready.
Last to skate.
I glided onto the ice,
music started.
I began my first spin,
I couldn't stop.
The time passed quickly.
I finished.
Applause and flowers thrown
on the ice.
I wasn't scared anymore.

*Sarah Griffin  (10)*
*Uffington Primary School*

## WHERE HAVE ALL THE PAPERCLIPS GONE?

Where have all the paperclips gone?
Don't ask me, maybe they have been
taken by a bumble bee!

Where have all the paperclips gone?
Maybe they have fallen down the drain.
Don't ask me, you're the one with the big brain.

Where have all the paperclips gone?
Maybe they're on the floor
or took off out the door!
We'd better find them before
the big old grumpy teacher comes!

*Stamp! Stamp! Stamp!*
Oh, oh, we're in trouble, the teacher is coming.

Children where have all the paperclips gone?
Miss, we don't know where the paperclips have gone
and we don't really care.
Just then we found the paperclips.
Guess where they were.
In Santa's pencil case!

*Jessica Scott  (9)*
*Uffington Primary School*


## SMELLY SHOE

One, two, smell my shoe,
Three, four, smell it some more.
Five, six, made you sick,
Seven, eight, made your mum faint.
Nine, ten, do it again.

*Kirsty McHardy  (9)*
*Uffington Primary School*

## TEN LITTLE SKITTLES

Ten little skittles sitting in a packet
one ran away because the others made a racket.

Nine little skittles sitting in the sun
one ran away because the other threw a bun.

Eight little skittles standing in the shed
one ran away because the others took his bed.

Seven little skittles standing on the floor
one ran away because life was such a bore.

Six little skittles standing in mid-air
one ran away because the others went to a fair.

Five little skittles climbing up a tree
one ran away because the others hurt his knee.

Four little skittles standing on a wall
one ran away because the others said he'd fall.

Three little skittles doing PE
one ran away because there came a buzzy bee.

Two little skittles doing drama
one ran away because the others took his armour.

One little skittle standing all alone
a big dog came along and took him home.

No little skittles standing anywhere
a boy came along and found the place bare!

*Larena Soper (10)*
*Uffington Primary School*

## FIVE SCOTTISH SOLDIERS

Five Scottish soldiers walking through a door,
The door fell apart, then there were four.

Four Scottish soldiers ran away to sea,
One got thrown overboard, then there were three.

Three Scottish soldiers went to the loo,
One never came back, then there were two.

Two Scottish soldiers using a gun,
One got shot, then there was one.

One Scottish soldier all alone,
Got really lonely and went off home.

No Scottish soldiers fighting on a field,
No more fighting for the rest of the world!

*Scott Macdonald  (11)*
*Uffington Primary School*


## THE SNOW POEM

A silent night in the town,
The snow starts falling on the ground,
Still, as the white snow falls on the ground,
Until the sun rises,
The town is not still anymore,
He started down the alleys,
The towns are silent and still,
He walked along a street of endless snow,
The snow was up to his ankles,
He was frozen right through.

*Charlotte Rayner  (9)*
*Uffington Primary School*

## THE MORNING FROST

The frozen ground,
Crispy and crunchy,
All around.

Everyone slipping and sliding,
On the freezing frost,
And the green grass hiding.

Water is frozen everywhere,
Hard as stone,
Trees are bare.

Gravestones have a hat of frost,
Standing still, lonely and lost.

*Charlotte Holley  (11)*
*Uffington Primary School*


## FROST

It's like a pure white landscape,
The sky is misty blue,
Leaves are spiky round the edge,
The ground looks like a white hedgehog,
The frost crunches like a boiling saucepan.
The molehills are frozen solid,
The leaves' veins stand out clearly,
Spiders' webs are all lit up,
Leaves glisten like Christmas trees.
Trees are bare, but they are going white,
Leaves die with the bitterness of the frost.

*Karen Cooper  (10)*
*Uffington Primary School*

## THE TOURNAMENT

I've been sitting for twenty minutes
Wondering what to write.
I've been given ten minutes for it,
I think that's really tight.
I was going to write about a football tournament
But I don't know where to start.
I know it all vaguely,
But I don't know some little parts.
I've been in a couple of matches before,
In fact quite a lot.
The first one I was defender,
Now I'm playing up front.
So we're going to play in this tournament
I can't even guess the scores.
We're going in at half term
With lots of other schools.
It's coming up to going away,
And I've been praying to the Lord
That we'll win on the day.

*Jack Baily  (10)*
*Uffington Primary School*


## FROST

Feet frozen to the ground
Not a sound,
No one at all around.

All trees bare
A cold breeze in the air.
Everything anchored to the spot.
It's everything but hot.

A rim of frost on a leaf,
The ice shines like a coral reef.
Spiders' webs sparkle in the sun
Soon it will go and then there will be none.

**Louise Sworn (11)**
**Uffington Primary School**


## THE PILLOW FIGHT

*Buff! Ow!*
I'm having a pillow fight with my brother.
He runs away.
I'm in hot pursuit.
*Bam!* I get him smack right on the back of the head.
He turns round and *wham!*
There's a collision between the pillows.
*Smack*, he gets me.
*Bam!* I get him back.
*Bam! Bang!*
He swings at me,
I duck, he misses.
*Ahh!* He's knocked my ornament off
'I'll get you,' I yell.
So here I am chasing him all around the house.
'I'll get you,' I keep saying.
I hide in a cupboard then jump out
and whack him on the head.
Off he goes screaming his head off,
it's over.
I've won.
I'm so happy that I won, yeah!

**Sophie Bowsher (10)**
**Uffington Primary School**

## WHERE HAVE ALL THE PAPERCLIPS GONE?

Where are all the paperclips?
They're not stuck to the ceiling or floating in the air,
They might be on a chair.
Are they under the table?
Are they in your pencil case
Or are they everywhere?
Who knows?
What am I going to do?
Every day I come to teach the class
and I write on the board.
Where have all the paperclips gone?
Where have they gone?
I come to school,
I can't get in,
School's closed.
I look through the window,
My class is full of paperclips.
I can't believe my eyes.

***Emma Rayner  (9)***
***Uffington Primary School***


## THE HORSE CHESTNUT

The horse chestnut
Has lovely green leaves.
It also has gorgeous looking conker shells,
Which are green and prickly,
They scratch and poke your hands.

But inside the conker shells however,
The smooth brown conker is sleeping soundly
Inside its velvet bed.

After a while the conkers wake up,
They all fall to the ground.
The children all run around the trunk,
Collecting them up.

The children all go home,
They polish their conkers,
They want their conker to be the best,
They want their conker to be the biggest,
Ready for school the next day.

*Margaret Tingey (11)*
*Wantage CE Junior School*


## WHAT IS RED?

Red is a cherry, juicy and sweet,
A spilt glass of wine
Staining the carpet,
Fire blazing into the sky.
Red is a ribbon, tied in your hair,
Red is blood dripping from your finger,
Your nose is red in icy-cold weather,
Red is a robin's chest,
Glossy and silky, soft and smooth.
Red is a warning saying *Stop!*
A ruby is a ring on your finger,
A red sunset turning the sky to fire,
A rose is red, a sweet smelling flower,
Red is your heart, thumping and beating, keeping you alive,
Red is a raspberry lolly, icy, cold and juicy,
Red is anger building up inside you,
Red is embarrassment, trying to hide,
Red is a warm feeling, making me feel happy.

*Laura Hickman (10)*
*Wantage CE Junior School*

## WHAT IS BLUE?

Blue is a colour,
Cooling you on a hot day.
A colour of a sparkling sapphire,
Glistening bright.
Blue is a blue-backed dolphin
Swimming in the sea,
And the colour of the sky is blue.
Ice is blue, a cold blue,
And is like running water,
Blue is a dark ink,
And a blue cartridge.
Blue gives you a feeling of cold, icy water,
Blue is a sparkling sapphire,
Shining on my fingers.

*Rebecca Sutton  (10)*
*Wantage CE Junior School*


## WHAT IS RED?

Red is the sun on a warm summer's day,
Red is anger bursting out of me,
Red is the sunset on a warm summer's eve,
Red is explosion coming from a volcano.

Red is fire, burning down a house,
I love red, it means everything to me,
Red is the poppy for remembering the war.

Red is Santa, coming down chimneys,
Red is my Swiss Army knife with gadgets on,
Red are poppies in a farmer's field,
What would we do without you, red?

*Sam Fox  (10)*
*Wantage CE Junior School*

## THE WILD OAK TREE

In the wild wind the crown was
Getting swayed,
The bottom was calm
And was agreeing with the wind
When the branches were waving
In the wind
The leaves were coming off onto
The road,
And cars,
Then it was more bare then ever
And you could see the branches
Like hands
And the big twisted
Trunk the branches came to the ground
And the roots were twisted even more
The trees looked like it would fall.

*Alan Easton  (10)*
*Wantage CE Junior School*


## THE TREE FOUNTAIN

The giant willow standing in the sun,
The thin leaves washing the sky,
In the wind blowing slowly,
The thin branches like vines,
Gushing and rustling in the breeze,
The tall trunk full of roots deep down,
The tree towering above,
Making shade on the ground,
The leaves spreading like a fountain,
The thick bark crinkled and hard.

*Stewart Hannah  (11)*
*Wantage CE Junior School*

## WHAT IS RED?

Red is fire burning and raging,
Scarlet is blood trickling from a cut,
A little life lost away,
Crimson-faced he can see only red,
A blind rage of anger and fury.

Scarlet the apple glossy and bright,
Juicy and tempting,
Red is a sunset,
Dying out of sight,
Rubies are shining a fortune.

Red are the leaves dead and falling,
Red is a jumper, uniform and all,
Red is *Stop!* on signs and lights,
Red is bold, shining and bright.

*Thomas Harris  (10)*
*Wantage CE Junior School*


## RACHEL'S BRIGHTLY COLOURED POPPY

It is attractive and bright,
        With colours of red,
        Pink, yellow and orange.

                Its petals spread out
        And curl round in the
                Spring and summer.

        The stem is fat
        And plump
In the summer it
  Sways in the wind.

*Rachel Bowers  (9)*
*Wantage CE Junior School*

## THE SEASON TREE

In autumn the wind is blowing
The trees fall with a tumble
And tumble down to the ground.
Waves of leaves crashing like thunder,
Lightning strikes,
Trees keep falling,
The forest is dying today.

In summer the trees just stand there happily, joyfully
Singing and swaying all through the day.

In winter leaves keep dying
Falling off trees turning crunchy.
They fall on the floor all dead
The winter is over, *hooray*, say the trees.

In spring the leaves grow back
And the trees live again.

*Lee Rutter  (11)*
*Wantage CE Junior School*


## WHAT IS GREEN?

Green are the leaves on a tree, on a bright summer's day,
Green is an emerald that dazzles green light,
Green is an apple, lush and juicy,
Green is when you're feeling sick or nervous,
Green makes you feel cool, relaxed and refreshed,
Green is a peppermint,
And a dark green pear,
Green is for the sea,
And the slimy, slippery seaweed.

*Ben Boden  (11)*
*Wantage CE Junior School*

## THE MAJESTIC OAK

A tall twisted trunk,
High above the ground,
Rough crinkled leaves,
Far below the crown,
Make the oak so grand,
There in the foreground.

The shade protects the travellers,
The sun dapples the trunk,
In the wood, forest or copse,
On the root, twig, trunk or bough,
The roots below absorb the water,
To make the leaves so green.

The bough that children swing on,
The majestic leaves flow down,
The branches high,
The roots so low,
Make the oak so real
With the mottled bough.

*Sam Withnall  (10)*
*Wantage CE Junior School*


## A WEEPING WILLOW

A weeping willow is like a
Waterfall on all sides,
The leaves start at the top,
And flow down to the bottom.

The branches are like
A fountain springing up,
And then falling down.

The trunk gets higher and higher,
First big boughs come,
Then long, twisted branches,
Then tiny crinkled twigs.

Then along comes man.
They saw and chop it down.
The sap slides and slithers out,
As if the tree is crying,
In agony and pain.

*Michael Donovan  (10)*
*Wantage CE Junior School*


## THE TREE IN SEASONS

The tree in winter,
Blowing in the wind,
When the snow falls,
The trunk stands
Bare and white.

The tree in spring,
Blowing gently;
The sun shining on
The leaves,
Warming the buds.

The tree in summer,
The big old tree,
Standing in the shade
Of the old town hall.

The tree in autumn,
The leaves crispy and brown
Falling to the ground.

*Natasha Valentine  (11)*
*Wantage CE Junior School*

## THE FOREVER GROWING TREE

The tall, twisted trunk,
Towering like an enormous giant,
With crinkled leaves weeping
On the green carpet below.

Almost like a giant rearing horse,
A dappled horse, looking for food,
The roots ready to trip over travellers,
Getting shade from the crown.

When the wind blows,
A fountain of leaves fall off,
But the tree with its forest of roots,
Still standing, forever growing.

Then the strong willow was found
Decaying on the floor,
Branches once strong and healthy
Now lying on the floor.

A hunter had come
And cut down the tree.
Not knowing how much
It meant to me.

*Jenny Leslie  (10)*
*Wantage CE Junior School*


## THE BIG OAK

Massive oak standing tall,
All the baby oaks look up and admire it.
The twisted roots anchoring into the ground,
The huge trunk stretching for a mile up high,
All the branches reaching up into the sky.

Man comes and chops down the big oak,
You think you can hear the others say,
*Why does man devour all the trees?*
In the distance you can hear a saw.
Do they know what they are doing
Killing helpless living things?

*Andrew Boyle  (10)*
*Wantage CE Junior School*


## THE WEEPING WATERFALL WILLOW

The weeping willow hanging down like a waterfall,
Its leaves swaying in the wind,
The crashing twigs hitting the ground,
The roots twisted and curly.

The leaves crinkled and rough,
The towering branches rise up in the sky,
With some prickly twigs that cut your hands,
The dappled trunk in the sunlight.

In summer, the crown sits on the top of the tree,
The insects and animals making their beds,
Warm and cosy at the top of the tree.

Autumn comes, the prickly leaves and twigs fall off,
Rough trees old and shabby,
Wood cracks and down come loose branches,
The wind makes the tree sway.

The rumble and tumble of twigs,
Fall off in bundles,
The roots turning and twirling on the ground,
The towering trunk leading up to the sky.

*Cheryl Chittock  (10)*
*Wantage CE Junior School*

# THE TREE

There is a tree
In next door's yard,
It's hard to climb,
Its bark is hard.
It's strong as steel
And very old -
300 years
Or so I'm told.

It reaches up
Towards a cloud,
And rests the birds
Upon its boughs.
It shelters me
When it starts to rain,
When you break a twig,
It bears the pain.

On autumn nights
The tree is there,
Silent, still
Its branches bare.
The snow soon comes,
With a blanket of white,
But still it just stands there,
Out of the light.

There is a tree
In next door's yard,
It's hard to climb,
Its bark is hard.
It's strong as steel,
And very old -
300 years
Or so I'm told.

*Nadia Walton  (11)*
*Wantage CE Junior School*


## ORANGE

What is orange?
Orange is,
The juicy fruit sitting in the pot,
Like the bright sun in the sky.

Orange are the nasturtiums
Waving in the wind,
Like hands waving goodbye.

In a flame there is orange,
Brilliant and burning hard
On the fire so bright.

The creeping marmalade cat,
Asleep by the fire,
Is gingery-orange,
Keeping warm by the blazing fire.

Orange is the big balloon
At the birthday party
Hanging on the wall
Big and bright.

*Kim Kelly  (11)*
*Wantage CE Junior School*

## WHAT IS BLUE?

Blue is aqua,
Cool and refreshing,
The sky on a cloudless day.
Blue are the waves,
Leaping high on a summer's day.
It is the colour of the deep
Dark oceans of mystery.
It is the river running free,
With the blue sky above.
Blue are the whales
Splashing and diving,
Swimming in their blue ocean.
Blue is a chill, a cold,
Blue is the icy-cold colour.

*Christopher Fellingham  (11)*
*Wantage CE Junior School*


## MY TREE

A long gigantic tree swaying in the wind,
Leaves and twigs, falling to the ground,
The twisted branches,
The roots searching for water,
Blossom hanging onto its branches,
The leaves waving in the air.

The leaves twinkle in the sun,
Some berries falling to the ground,
Leaves waving in the wind,
The solid trunk looking for sunlight,
A big forest of lovely gigantic trees.

*Jordan Molyneux  (11)*
*Wantage CE Junior School*

## THE OLD HOUSE

The old house stands aged and crumbling,
A builder's nightmare, a plumber's frightmare,
Whenever I pass that lonely place,
It seems to stare at me with its old grey face.

As I walk along the street,
I see the fencing tall and neat,
Even that seems to look at me,
Through its elderly history.

Most would be horrified to live in there,
Except the lady with grey-white hair,
Some say she's mad you see,
But I think it would be a lovely house for me!

*Harry Coules (10)*
*Wantage CE Junior School*


## THE HORSE CHESTNUT TREE

The great horse chestnut tree -
Standing straight and strong,
But beyond that where you can't see
Are little buds ready to unfurl
And when they do . . .
A tiny little white or pink flower appears,
Then slowly they begin to turn into spiky, green cases.
Then in autumn these green *mines* drop off
And out of its soft satin case falls
A shiny, round, smooth, brown gem stone.
When the rain falls on it a pink root grows.
Then a green shoot sprouts.
As the years go by the gemstone turns into another tree.

*Daniel Monnery (11)*
*Wantage CE Junior School*

## WHAT IS BLUE?

Blue is the colour of dolphins, splashing,
Happily, calling to each other.
Blue is the colour of Scotland's rugby shirts,
Or a trickling stream, rushing downhill.
A blue river gently crossing the countryside
On a hot summer's day.
Blue is a colour in a rainbow, proudly with the others.
Blue ink blotches on the paper.

Dazzling blue crystal in the rock,
Blue tulips growing in the field,
Blue is the colour of a knight's shield,
Glinting in the sun.
Blue is the colour of a cloudless sky,
Blue is cold on a winter's day,
Chelsea's kit is blue as the sky.

*Ross Kerr (10)*
*Wantage CE Junior School*


## ANDREW'S PINK SURPRISE

The pink petals curl towards
The sunlight,
The stem is busy collecting
Minerals and water,
Bees go back and forward
Collecting nectar.

The velvet petals observe
The sun,
Insects buzz or crawl over,
The nectar covers the stem.

*Andrew Bennett (10)*
*Wantage CE Junior School*

## HANNAH'S WILD LILY

The pink and purple petals are
Waving to all the other flowers
The colours stream into one another.

The buzzy bee comes along to
Smell the lovely flowers
And take the pollen.
The buzzy bee lands with a
Thump on the smooth, silky stamens.
Off the bee flies to another flower.

The stalk is pure green with
Juicy, squashy dew running down.
The flower is rather tired by
Now and glad the day is over.

*Hannah Blow  (10)*
*Wantage CE Junior School*


## ANNIE'S GARDEN PURPLE

The long purple petals lean onto the stalk.
They are so bright and colourful,
With their bright yellow stamens.
It's a rich purple and blue with velvety petals.
It's tall, thin and has lots of powdery pollen
Which attracts the bees.
The flower is fed on water.
The bugs and insects creep quietly around,
On the rounded rich purple petals.
While the black and orange bees
Buzz around collecting pollen,
The flower grows secretly more every day.

*Annie Berrett  (10)*
*Wantage CE Junior School*

## The Seasons Of The Oak

The year has started,
Spring has sprung,
The birds make a nest,
Leaves of all shades of green
Pop out of buds.

The summer, a beautiful time,
An oak stands alone,
The heat warms him,
The birds start to sing.

Now autumn is here,
The leaves turn to gold,
People run through the leaves,
Crunch, crunch, crunch.

Winter is on the oak,
The oak is stripped bare,
An animal brushes past,
Twigs snap everywhere.

*David Oakes  (10)*
*Wantage CE Junior School*


## What Is Red?

Red is a juicy apple in the breeze,
Red is hot when you burn your knees.
Red is fire blazing bright,
Red is a ruby shimmering in sight.

Red is a shirt of Man United,
Red is the cross on England's flag.
Red is blood as it pours from your hand,
Red is a cockerel's crest way up high.

Red is anger,
Red is embarrassment.
Red is the lightsaber of Darth Vader, evil.
Red is a ball, big and round.

Red is a sunset on a summer's evening,
Red is a rose in the summer.
Red is Santa as he flies across the sky,
Red is the sun big and bright.

*Stuart Chaplin  (10)*
*Wantage CE Junior School*

## BLUE

What is blue?
Blue is a big juicy blueberry,
A blue sapphire glistening with pride,
A bright blue summer's sky with
No clouds in sight.

Blue is a good tempered sea,
Big blue dolphins diving in the
Blue ocean.
Little blue teardrops running down my cheek.
A blue background on the St Andrew's flag.

Blue is the colour of Chelsea's
Football kit.
Blue are my hands covered in ink,
Blue is a cold and icy colour.

*Jane Cameron  (10)*
*Wantage CE Junior School*

## KAYLEIGH'S HARMONY

Rich peach petals,
Trying to reach the sun,
Bright yellow stamens,
Attracting all the bees.

The sweet fragrance from the petals,
The sweetest you can smell,
The tall green stalks,
Delivering all the food.

Velvety smooth petals,
Are the beauty of the flower,
As the dusk falls
The flower goes to sleep.

*Kayleigh Walton  (10)*
*Wantage CE Junior School*


## GIANT SHINY CONKER

Once a year, every autumn,
On the horse chestnut tree,
Spiky green cases fall from the branches,
Bringing shiny conkers for me.

Through the branches when I look up,
I see a mass of tiny holes,
Sun glistening through them every one,
The leaves like tiny bowls.

The towering gnarled trunk,
Twisting branches and twigs,
Conker shells litter the paths and road,
More falling from the boughs.

*Lisa Golding  (11)*
*Wantage CE Junior School*

## WHAT A WASTE

It towers above everything else,
Never wavering,
Going straight up.

Exotic birds flutter in its majestic branches,
Monkeys hop from bough to bough,
Chameleons laze in the sunlight,
Feeding on the tasty insects.

Its roots spread deep into the ground,
Soaking up every drop of water.
Its lovely fruit falls from great heights,
Dropping to the ground to feed other animals.

All of a sudden, a terrible noise comes,
Voices say, 'Look at this one, Bert,'
Animals flee, but not all,
The humans start up chain-saws,
*Vroom, slice, chop, groan, creak. Timber!*

It plummeted to the ground,
*Crash!*
Animals' homes destroyed in one fell swoop,
Only the stump is left.

Mashed up into paper to be written on,
Turned into furniture,
You could be sitting on it,
You could be writing on it,
And at the end of the day it's thrown away.
Wasted . . .

*Ian Bridgeman (10)*
*Wantage CE Junior School*

## LOVELY LADY

Creeping up above the sky
Two tiny leaves peep
Day by day growing larger
Then one sunny morning in spring
A bud appeared
A green bud short and fat
Then suddenly pop! out comes a flower
A beautiful flower, peach and lilac
That softly fades slowly into each other
The spiky yellow stamens point toward the sky
A bee lands slowly and drinks the nectar
While picking up the pollen
Then the sun begins to set
The little flower closes up for another day.

*Esther Knight  (10)*
*Wantage CE Junior School*


## CREAMY STAR

Rich petals curled towards the sun,
Encouraging insects to its smooth petals,
A tall stalk going up,
Carrying water and minerals.

Sun attracts the creamy flower up,
Bees buzz to and fro,
Fluttering wings excitedly,
Settling on a yellow stamen.

Closing down to sleep,
Curling in his cream petals,
The bees drift away.
Goodnight creamy star.

*Rhianna Drury  (10)*
*Wantage CE Junior School*

## THE KENYA SURPRISE

The Kenya surprise,
It smells really nice,
The petals look gorgeous,
It even grows spice.
It now grows in England,
Far from its home,
In someone's back garden,
All on its own.

*Michael Bellis  (10)*
*Wantage CE Junior School*


## CHARLEY'S POPPY

The petals are curly and bright,
The stamens are thin, tall and yellow.
The stalk has to have food to live,
The yellow attracts the bees.
The petals are rich and smooth.

*Charley Offill  (9)*
*Wantage CE Junior School*

# THE HAZY BEACH

People lay their worn-out deck-chairs against the old frustrated wall,
The wall cracked and gnarled on the edges like a twisted old tree.
The people content to relax chilled in the coolness of the shadow.

Pebbles feel gritty, lumpy and irritating underfoot.
Gulls cackling in a chorus of echoes, each sounding like a scream
    with no effort
Ending abruptly with a swoop or glide.

The faces stare. Some friendly and cheerful, some with unreadable
    expressions that appear as dark as ink.
The waves now closer, thunder like an orchestra of drums
    in the distance.
The breeze blows gracefully onto the shore, it sounds like an old
    man's tired whistle.
The moist sand is licked affectionately by the tip of the salty water.

A sudden wisp of ice wrung wind glides over the pebbles as if
    it were a tissue twisting and writhing in mid-air.
The frail fingers of seaweed bob their heads up to catch a breath
    of fresh air,
Their bodies are washed away like limp pieces of string.
The people glance up undisturbed,
Then go back to a brown crumpled old newspaper,
    crackling in the wind.

By the water.
It retreats like a forlorn army accepting defeat.
At first it gives a sharp tingling sensation but soon becomes
    dry and soothing.

The shells by the water's edge are crisp and grimy, sinking deeply
    into the soft sand.
Different sounds drifting, gently settling in the distance.
The hustle and bustle of the pier visible as it walks out to sea
    on its giant brown legs.

The rocks out at sea look like mosaics of shattered glass,
Each one a fragment of the once beautiful cliff.
On the far-off horizon, the sun's rich gaze is reflected on
the glittering ocean like a gleaming mountain range.
Left forever in peace.

*Jonathan Holmes  (11)*
*Witney CP School*


## LUXURY BEACH

I stand high above the beach
the sun bursts through the clouds.
I hear the sea roaring in the distance.
Walking onto the beach
with my shoes in one hand
sunglasses in the other
I stand still.
Wet towels over my head
blowing in the wind.
As I walk further a gust of wind blows into my face,
the sea gets louder.
Some women sitting on the sand,
are talking and laughing.
As I move on,
two women are reading an article out of a newspaper.
I lick my lips as I taste the salt.
I go up to the sea, put my toe in it, it feels cool.
I then decide to walk along the edge of the water.
People in the background getting further away.
Now the sun sets,
it gets cooler,
the sea calms down,
as I walk off the beach.

*Gemma Barber  (11)*
*Witney CP School*

## EMERALD BEACH

I looked down on the golden crisp sand,
Children splashing in the sea with the rolling of waves.
I stepped down with the scorching sand tickling my feet.
I hear the gentle flapping of towels on a line,
I hear the people chatting, the children laughing.
The roar of the sea is getting louder.
The waves crashing down like thunderbolts
On the rocks and pebbles on the seabed.
I stride forward like a knight in shining armour,
Suddenly the sea gushes forward like an army,
Burying my feet with wet sloppy sand.
I step back, the dazzling sun scorching my back,
I walk on down the beach, fading in the salty mist
                              of the emerald green sea.

*Jonathan Heath  (10)*
*Witney CP School*


## THE BEATING SOUNDS

The crashing of the waves, flowing onto the beach,
The sun beaming down on me, flashing into my eyes.
The smooth feeling of the sand brushing on my feet,
Is slowly turning into the roughness of the shells and pebbles.
Seagulls squealing in the sky above me, blending in with the sea.
The chattering of the people around, with the towels
                              flapping above me.
Turning newspaper pages crackling.
The sand gradually starting to get stones in it.
When I look up the waves crash onto the shore,
Then, they gradually bubble up to the tip of my toes.

*Helen Bloomfield  (10)*
*Witney CP School*

## SWIRLING, SWISHING SEA

As I stand staring out to sea I hear the muffled babble as
it runs backwards and forwards across the stony shore.

There are people resting lazily in old creaking deck-chairs
as they chatter loudly about their day.

Gentle gusts of wind blow silently through the clear blue sky.
The blazing sun is reflected in the rippling, broken sea.

Seagulls cry far off in the distance, calling to one another
as they swoop across the giant, roaring waves.

As I walk over the smooth pebbles and shingle they crunch
loudly and washing flaps violently above in the breeze.

People's conversations are louder and the sea is not muffled.
It crashes loudly on the beach washing up huge clumps of seaweed.

I wander further down the beach. Two women are lying in the sun
and they are flicking quickly through a tatty old newspaper.

The sea roars and I can smell the fresh sea air rising from
the foam-topped waves and I taste the sea salt on my dry lips.

Background noises are fading. The huge waves fall and crash upon
the beach like thunder then cowardly rushes back.

Now I am inches away from the sea. It roars loudly like a huge
monster lashing violently backwards and forwards.

The sea crashes once more against the shore and then rolls
back again. Every other sound is washed away by the rumbling sea.

Only the roaring of the sea can be heard as it crashes wildly
on the pebble beach then cowardly babbles away again.

Then I walk slowly down the shoreline staring out at the horizon.

*Emma Bowles  (11)*
*Witney CP School*

## A SUNNY BEACH

I see the waves crashing into foam
as they hit the rocks.
I'm getting hot so I take my shoes off
and jump onto the soft silky sand below.
I can feel the grit from the sand in between my toes.
I hear the towels flapping in the wind above my head.
I walk towards two ladies chatting to one another on the sand.
I'm getting closer to the sea now, I can feel the salty sea air
on my face and in my hair.
The seagulls screech to each other.
I tip my toe into the sea, then I walk in a bit deeper.
Then without warning a big wave rushes up my legs,
the sea is icy-cold, so I walk slowly back onto the beach.
I walk heading for the pier as the noise gets fainter and fainter,
all I can hear are the waves splashing and the seagulls calling.
I look back and I can see the sun setting in the distance.

*Lucy Joanna Ellis  (10)*
*Witney CP School*


## THE HORIZON

Hear the loud crashing of the
gentle soft waves.
Smell the salty sea air.
Feel my feet sinking softly into the hot sand.
Care about nothing.
Walk slowly towards the salty crashing water.
Step silently onwards into the cold blue sea.
Look out to the horizon.
The water gently lapping back and forth
over my toes!
Silence!

*Sarah Howkins  (10)*
*Witney CP School*

## SEASIDE POEM

Sound of seagulls in the sky calling to each other.
The sound of the sea roaring like thunder.
The smell of the seaweed blows through the air.
The feeling of the pebbles scuttling under my feet
like I am walking across a railway track.
The taste of salt water lands on my tongue.
The sea scuttling across the stony ground
as it fades away into the distance.
I hear children in the background,
slowly fades away,
and people talking as I walk past
the flapping washing lines,
and as I walk back to the town
the sound of the beach slowly fades away.

*Stuart Batts  (10)*
*Witney CP School*


## THE JUNGLE

Moist warm air floods around me
The long grass brushes against my legs
I can see a tiger prowling in the undergrowth
I can smell the plants around me
I can hear a monkey screech as a parrot flies
overhead squawking.
There's a small clear stream near my feet,
I take a drink.
I splash some on my face, the lovely cool water
runs down my face.
The rain begins to fall, I take shelter under
gigantic leaves.
I can hear the rain tapping on the leaf.

*Thomas Smith  (11)*
*Witney CP School*

## BEACH POEM

I can hear the seagulls squawking,
and the noise of the roaring sea
and feel the wind as it touches my cold ears.

I hear the towels flapping in the air
and feel the coldness of the water on my feet
as I step into the cold water.

I can taste the salty water as I get
nearer the water.

I hear the people chattering and laughing
and the noise of pages being turned.

I hear the noise of the sea crashing
against the rocks.

As I walk further away from the beach
I can faintly hear the noise of the
people laughing and the noise of the
roaring sea.

*Matthew Brocks  (11)*
*Witney CP School*

## THE PEBBLE BEACH

I walk down the hot golden path.
I feel a warm gentle breeze faintly touching my skin.
The sun is crashing against the pebbles down on the beach.

I reach the beach, the warm pebbles touch my feet.
The heat warms me up.
As I walk closer to the sea I smell hot dogs sizzling in the pan.

I can hear people having conversations in the background.
I am just about to put my toe into the water,
a shiver tingles down my spine.

I can taste the salt from the sea.
As I walk back towards the golden path,
I buy a hot dog.
My sandals in one hand, my hot dog in the other,
I walk up the warm golden path.

*Shelly Allday (10)*
*Witney CP School*


## SUMMER'S BEACH

I am standing on a balcony overlooking the beach,
I hear people chattering and the sea crashing
against the pebbles.

I feel the sun beating down on my face,
I feel the smooth pebbles against my feet.
As I walk to the sea
I hear people's beach towels flapping in the wind.

In the distance I hear a boat coming in from
a long night's fishing.
The sea is getting louder as I get nearer.

A woman nearby says 'The sun is nice and hot'
The sea is getting louder still.
A man says 'Good morning' to me as I walk past.

I feel the sea lashing against my feet.
I also hear an amusement park faraway.
I walk along the seashore and all I can hear is the sea.

*Laura O'Shea (10)*
*Witney CP School*

## PEBBLE BEACH

The smooth pebbles rub on my bare feet.
I can hear the faint roar of the waves.
I can taste the salty sea on the top of my tongue.
I can hear people talking about the dreadful stories
from the newspaper.
I can see a child eating some chips.
I am putting my feet in the silky cold sea.
The cold sea cools me down.
I can hear the faint sounds of the towels
flapping and the arcade music
as I back away from the sea.
I am walking on the shore now,
I hear the seagulls.
The sea is getting fainter,
now I am leaving the beach,
where the smooth pebbles rubbed
my bare feet and the sea roared once before.

*Kadie Foster  (10)*
*Witney CP School*


## BEACH POEM

The sea crashes against the pebbles.
The pebbles are very hot and it feels like my feet are on fire.
The seagulls sing to one another and go to float calmly on top
of the surface of the ocean.
I walk under some towels, they flick water at me as they dry.
The sea gets louder and louder as I come nearer and nearer.
I can hear the music on the pier where the amusements are.
The noises behind me are all starting to fade into the background.
I put my toe in the water and I bring it back because it is cold.
I walk down the coastline and all I can hear is the sea and the seagulls.

*Ralph Rankin  (11)*
*Witney CP School*

## SUNSET BEACH

I am coming to a beach where the sea
sparkles in the sunlight.
I walk along the pebbles all shiny and smooth.
I carry on walking and hear people
laughing and chatting.

Seagulls squawking and fighting over food
that people have dropped.
The wind is blowing the towels across my face
as I walk further.
The waves are getting louder as the sea
smell wafts across my face.

I can see a beautiful sunset far away
with the horns of ships hooting in the distance.
I come to the sea edge watching all the bright
shells being swept out to sea by the waves
looking like beautiful treasures.

I step into the sea with the ice-cold waves
crashing against my feet.
The sound of people's voices getting quieter
and quieter but the sea is getting more vicious and noisy.

As I step away the sea seems to come closer
and closer to me.
I walk back, more people have arrived
as it is getting hotter.

I feel drops of rain on my cheeks
as I look up and see a colourful rainbow,
the perfect ending of a perfect day.

*Joshua Long  (10)*
*Witney CP School*

## SUMMER BEACH

A muffled roar reaches my ears.
I turn to see a beach with shimmering
sea and glimmering pebbles.
The hot sun on my back as my feet
touch the smooth pebbles.
Gulls circling and squawking above my head.
Wind blowing around me,
spray filling my face and mouth.
The salty taste as I walk towards
the diamond sea.
Waves tipped with foam,
like lace on blue velvet,
run over the pebbles towards me,
then curling up and backing away.
I walk along the shore.
The sun dips.
I am in a warm golden light.
The sun reflects on the sea.
The horizon shimmering, as the scene fades away . . .

*Charlotte Bond  (10)*
*Witney CP School*

## BEACH POEM

I step down into the photo
I hear the sea roaring
The sound of the waves crashing on the ground
I am walking across the hard, pebble beach
with the wind blowing fast.

The sound of the flapping towels above my head
I walk past two people talking
The sun beating down
The sea is roaring louder as I get closer
I can hear the amusements on the pier
as I move closer.

I walk along the beach with my feet
in the cold sea salt water
Then I go back past the people talking
and the flapping of the towels back out of the photo.

*Stephanie Hadfield  (11)*
*Witney CP School*

# BEACH POEM

As I walked closer
I started to hear the joy in the crowds nearby
I carried on walking
I saw the happiness in their eyes
I walked closer
I smelt the salty welcoming air
I got even closer
And the cool breeze ran through my hair
I was so close now
That I could see the sparkling blue sea
I carried on walking
I felt the soft silky sand that stuck to my feet
I was so close now that I just walked into the sea
I felt the cool water that just eased me to my knees
Then I realised
The sun was starting to set
I had so much fun that I didn't want to go so . . .
I called out to the person
I loved most of all.

*Pratik Patel (10)*
*Witney CP School*

## PEBBLE BAY

Sunshine beams down on me,
sea roaring while crashing to the shore.
Hard pebbles bristle my feet,
the sea looks like a bright sky of clouds,
people's towels sway in the wind,
spraying water over me.
People chattering, eating their sandy sandwiches,
sounds of newspaper pages turning over,
people still chattering in the background.
I come to some seats which are red and white,
they look like candy sticks,
seagulls squealing.
Sea roaring even louder as soft salty sea sprays
into my face.
I walk into the sea, the soft cold water touches
my feet, it cools me down.
The calm breeze blows on my face,
like a warm soothing feeling.
The calm sea sways left to right,
left to right, as I walk across the shore.

*Chris Kingston  (10)*
*Witney CP School*